MY CHARLIE BROWN LIFE
A Spiritual Autobiography

Debi Staples

Staples, Debi
ISBN: 978-1-7344205-1-7
My Charlie Brown Life: A Spiritual Autobiography / Debi
Staples – 2nd ed.

Cover art by Tracy Deptuck

Printed in the USA

MY CHARLIE BROWN LIFE

TABLE OF CONTENTS

PART III
"Good Grief"

FOREWORD BY
ED DE SOUSA

When one has acquired enough years in a life to measure it in multiple decades, something interesting happens in the brain. The chemical combinations and synapses fire off in random directions, often resulting in unpredictable and unimaginable thought processes. Some of us are apt to act on those impulses and, perhaps, become astronauts or deep sea divers. Others of us store up those impulses, leading otherwise quiet lives, saving up the extra electrical energy for later in life, when we can let loose their power in controlled bursts of genius. To be sure, Debi is a member of the latter group, like a great ship heading down a known path, yet having collected a large cargo of inspiration in the decades she has been at sea. It has been my great fortune to have made her acquaintance for some of that journey. "Steady as she goes" could always be heard called out from the captain's deck, but I always suspected that below decks lied the real treasure: the faithful carrying of decades' worth of life experiences, then to be examined by whomever was lucky enough to venture into the cargo hold.

In "My Charlie Brown Life," Debi grants us permission to go below decks as she reveals the nuggets of treasured experiences few have had an opportunity to see... until now. We find, as she shines a light on these events, that not only is there more to her than meets the eye, but it may also be true that we share some of those exact same experiences, however nuanced in our own history. That notion makes them comfortable to us, endearing the author to us and making us feel privileged for her having shared the decades with us and the thought processes that brought us all to today.

It seems true that for all sensitive and caring souls carrying such a cargo of experiences, there comes a time when we feel we have amassed so many stories that the time comes to unload them in some purposeful fashion. Debi has done that here with her recounting of her history, not just a "brain dump" but, rather, a reasoned and understandable evolution from childhood to thoughtful storyteller. And we, as witness to that transformation – and despite her admission that, at times, her life seems to be quite ordinary – are forced to admit, when we reach the end of her accounting, that each piece of her life was honed and crafted so meticulously as to produce a very extraordinary individual, more like a finely-tuned engine than a misdirected concoction of unrelated parts. Even when held under a microscope, the Charlie Brown character is far more complex than the reader is asked to believe at the start of her words. So the same can be said of Debi herself, and the reader must relent in acceptance of her uniqueness.

"My Charlie Brown Life" is a thought-provoking jaunt through one life that the author sees as ordinary, yet is anything but. Happily, the journey for Debi is not over yet, with more interesting stories to tell.

INTRODUCTION

Some of the fondest memories of my childhood were of my family and I gathering together in the living room to watch one of the Charlie Brown* holiday specials on television. The escapades of Charlie Brown and the gang (aka Peanuts) didn't have the children rebelling against their parents, nor were they full of the typical non-stop action, violence or sex of today's standard fare for kids. Charles Schultz, the creator of the Charlie Brown comic strip, had a vision for his work, and he did not compromise on that vision, even when his series ventured into the land of television.

The Charlie Brown was simply about a young boy, his friends, and his dog. Charlie Brown was an ordinary kid. He had a younger sister, Sally, who tried her best to defend her big brother from those who criticized him, sometimes wondering how he could be so dense about most of the things that mattered to her. Then there is Linus, Charlie Brown's best friend, confidante and sidewalk philosopher, who always tried to see the best in people. And we can't forget Lucy, Linus' older sister, who had her own strong sense of values and opinions on just about every subject, and she wasn't afraid to show it. And of course we can't mention Charlie Brown without including his irascible dog Snoopy, who was the perfect comic relief of the group.

So how it is that Charlie Brown has endeared himself to us through the generations? I believe it is because we can all relate to those ordinary moments we've shared in the comic book and on the small screen. I think that every one of us, young and old alike, could find something to relate to in one or more of the peanuts gang.

As I grew older, and life began to come at me from all sides, slamming me back every time I began to feel as if I had a foothold on things, I began to relate more and more to Charlie Brown. One of Charlies Brown's most famous quotes comes to mind as I write this: "I think I'm afraid to be happy, because whenever I get too happy, something bad happens." That is exactly how I started to feel! Especially when each bad thing seemed to come in pairs of twos and threes, one right after the other, as if the Universe was daring me to give happiness another chance. If Lucy had given me the advice she gave Charlie Brown, that "You learn more if you lose," then I would have given her the same comeback that he did, namely, "Well then, I must be the smartest person in the world."

I couldn't tell you how many times I've said what Charlie Brown would so often say when something had gone wrong in his life... only more often than not "Good grief" was not quite strong enough of a statement, as time and again I would find myself on my back after kicking out at the proverbial football that Lucy used to taunt Charlie Brown with every Thanksgiving.

The hard knocks of my life began to become so frequent that instead of crying or falling into a fit of despair, I would smile, shake my head and say "I am living a Charlie Brown life." I began to wonder if I would ever be truly happy... or at the very least, comfortable with who I was and where my life seemed to be going.

But of course, like with Charlie Brown, life wasn't all bad. It had its good times as well as the not-so-good. Put them all together and that's what makes up a life, after all. That is why I named my autobiography "My Charlie Brown Life." Thus far, like with Charlie Brown, my life has been quite ordinary. I do not have a high-powered job or know any famous people. I have not traveled the world or won any awards. I've certainly done nothing of enough note to warrant my own reality TV show. But as I look back on half century of life, I have started to notice various instances where people and events have tested and honed me into the person I am today, steering me in the direction I was meant to go in order for me to learn and grow… and become the best person I was meant to be. And amazingly enough, most of those lessons that I learned happened in *ordinary* moments, many of which I did not even notice as important or meaningful until they had passed.

Ironically, I never thought of Charlie Brown as a tragic figure; just a kid trying to find his way in this life, like the rest of us.

Ever since I was twelve years old, I took my spirituality very seriously. While most of my friends were concerned with the latest fashions, the newest rock band, or the hottest young movie star, one of my biggest passions was discovering who I was in relationship to God… though of course I didn't think of what I was doing in those terms at the time. Every word I said, every thought I had, every action I took, I reviewed in my head to see how it would look to others... then I felt anguish over how it would look to God. Whenever I fell from grace (aka sinned), which was often, I would try to find a way to justify myself to God… and of course, apologize profusely. Yet I was not a bad kid by any stretch of the imagination.

Every time I attended a church service, I would come out of the building feeling worse about myself then when I went in, as I was once again reminded that I was a sinner and that I would never reach perfection in God's eyes (as only Jesus was perfect). Whenever I tell one of my friends about this, they seem to feel sorry for me. They'd explain how their faith gives them such comfort. Oh, how I wished it had done the same for me! Yet at the same time, whenever they tell me this, I can tell they are still suffering… from doubts, guilt, and from trying to hide their sins from the rest of world (if not from themselves as well).

But now, looking back, I am glad I didn't find such comfort during those church services, because that would have made me complacent, causing me to follow the crowd without thinking for myself. I would rather think of myself as Linus did when he would sit patiently in that pumpkin patch, waiting for the Great Pumpkin to arrive, while the rest of his friends went off trick-or-treating. Linus didn't mind being left out of the crowd, because he was following his heart. It didn't matter to him if everyone else believed or not. Though of course he always hoped that his friends would join him.

But whereas I used to feel as if there was something wrong with me for what I believed, now I can embrace who I am without reservation. Some may look on my life with pity, or otherwise judge me... that is the risk I took the moment I decided to pen my autobiography... but I do not for one moment regret being true to myself.

Care to join me in the pumpkin patch for a while?

Charlie Brown first appeared in 1947, three years before Peanuts started, in a comic strip by Charles M. Schulz called Li'l Folks. He later appeared in the first Peanuts comic strip on October 2, 1950. A series of televised specials began airing in 1965.

PART I

"It's the Great Pumpkin, Charlie Brown"

"Most psychiatrists agree that sitting in a pumpkin patch is excellent therapy for a troubled mind."
LINUS

1

A Wonderfully Boring Childhood

"Do you think God cares?"
CHARLIE BROWN

I was born 3 days early. I've always joked that that was the only time in my life I've ever been early. (I prefer being on time or fashionably late to having to hurry up and wait.) My parents named me after an actress who was popular at the time – Debbie Reynolds. I've always thought it was cool to be named after an actress, since all through high school I had dreamed of becoming one myself. But I didn't want to be an actress for the fame, or even for the money. To me that was the best way to escape the boredom of my own life; and what better way than to put yourself in someone else's shoes for a while?

The only significant thing about my birth was that I was born without a hip socket. I had to wait for it to grow in so that I wouldn't walk with a limp for the rest of my life. This meant that for my first two years, I had to wear a brace that kept the lower half of my body confined. This brace also kept my legs turned out to the side. I do not remember this, but I've been told that I didn't let it bother me; I would happily stand up in my playpen with my legs bent out to the side, much like a sumo wrestler, and play without complaint. And when the brace finally came off, I skipped crawling and went straight to walking. Today the only physical evidence of this are two small dots under my chest where the brace was secured. Oh, and I have a slight wiggle to my walk... something my husband has always appreciated.

An unfortunate side effect of this experience is that once I began to move around in the brace, my family often felt sorry for me. So they compensated by feeding me – a lot. I still remember watching one of those old black and white 8mm home movies my uncle would take when the family would get together… and there I'd be, going from place to place around the dinner table, being fed something off of everyone's plate. Ironically, I wasn't a heavy baby, as I soon made up for those first two years of inactivity by being quite an active toddler. But I will forever equate food with the comforts of home, safety and acceptance. And the constant battle with my weight has been ongoing ever since.

Even so, I'm happy to say that I had a wonderfully boring childhood. I realize this may seem like an oxymoron, but today, when so many children are growing up in broken homes, I was blessed to grow up with two parents who loved me and stayed together. I grew up in a time of VHS and cassette tapes; before the Internet was a household name; when cancer was rare enough that we referred to it as "the big C"; when the worst thing a young girl had to worry about when she started dating was getting pregnant or contracting an STD; and when cell phones hadn't been invented yet… or if they had, no one we knew owned one. It was the time when everyone watched the same prime-time TV shows every night, drive-ins were still cool to go to, and the entire family had to share one phone. Heck, I still listened to The Beatles on my mother's 33's on the turn table in my room from time to time.

I know that every person over 50 has said that they grew up in a "simpler time," but I have no doubt that anyone who was born before the 1990's *did* live a much simpler life than kids do today. And I will forever be grateful for that.

When I was in second grade, my family and I moved from the big city to a small town, where we lived on a cul-de-sac (a street with a circle at the end of it) where everyone knew each other – and each other's' business. We never locked our doors at night. My mother was a stay-at-home mom, so we took our lunch boxes to school each day and dinner was always on the table at 5pm on weekdays. Friends and neighbors would come and go from our house nearly every day, and there was always coffee, Kool-Aid and homemade bread or cookies to share. When I got a bit older, we were the only house on the street to have a pool, so that was where most of the neighborhood kids would spend the hot summer days. I did well in school. I was never bullied. And there were always presents under the Christmas tree, no matter how tight money might have been that year. I have memories of numerous pets, family picnics, summer vacations at the beach, snow forts and sleep-overs. Even today, when I no longer live in the same state where I was born, my father still lives in the house I grew up in.

Until I was five, I even had an imaginary friend. I do not remember his name or what sort of creature he was, but apparently he was very important to me. I used to instruct my mother to set a place at the dinner table for him to eat with us and my mother had to say goodnight to him as well before I would go to sleep each night. I do not remember much more about him, sad to say.

My pediatrician told my parents that having an imaginary friend was a sign of intelligence, so they didn't try to persuade me that he wasn't real. And of course eventually I grew out of that phase, the same as I did my childhood blankie (much like with Linus, that blue blankie went with me everywhere). But today as I look back on it, I can't help but wonder if that imaginary friend wasn't so imaginary after all. Perhaps he was my guardian angel, who I could see, in my innocence, while others could not.

I was even lucky enough to believe in Santa Claus until I entered the 4th grade, when one of my classmates rudely informed me that he didn't exist. I realize that today most children already know that Santa Claus isn't real at a much younger age, but I will always cherish those years where for one month the world would become a magical place.

Once I knew that Santa Claus wasn't real, I started to find conspiracies all over the place. I once told a whole line of children at the mall that the Easter bunny, whose lap I was sitting on, was a girl, since I could see inside her costume (those head masks were always much too large for the person inside). And I didn't even believe in dinosaurs because the Bible never mentioned them, so I figured the school was lying to us about their existence.

Perhaps this was truly where my spiritual journey began, as I was learning not to take things at face value. But it would take me many years to return to a place where I believed that the world was a magical place.

Being born without a hip socket shaped my life in more ways than one. Because of being confined in a brace for the first 2 years of my life, my parents – in their desire to comfort me – fed me more than they probably should have, making it so that I will forever equate food with comfort, home and family. But it has also made it so that I cannot sleep without pressure on the lower half of my body. While some people need a night light on, or can't sleep on a certain side of the bed, I have to have some weight on my legs and feet, no matter how hot it may be, or I will not sleep. This also makes traveling especially difficult for me, as sleeping in a strange bed without the necessary weight has given me many sleepless nights.

2
BROKEN

I have a philosophy that has been refined
in the fires of hardship and struggle…
'Live and let live!'
LUCY

As a general rule, religion is supposed to be a source of comfort for those who practice it. Knowing there is something out there that is bigger than yourself; some powerful being who can smite your enemies while giving you rewards in the afterlife; a source of comfort to pray to in times of trouble; a place where you know exactly what is expected of you… that is what most people look for in a deity that they worship. In theory, religion should be a *positive* force in one's life.

But ever since religion was introduced into my life I could not help but feel as if I was somehow broken. Because I could not follow all the rules there were to follow. There was just no way that I could live up to God's impossibly high standards. According to what I was taught in the Bible (and in Sunday School) about how God worked and what God felt about me, I was basically born a sinner and would die a sinner, and if I played my cards right, asking for forgiveness before I could sin again, I might end up in Heaven as opposed to the fires of Hell with the devil for all eternity. I am speaking from the point of view of someone who was brought up as a Protestant Christian, but from what I've learned from others who were brought up in different religions, their feelings of inadequacy in regards to a higher power (aka God) usually stemmed from what they were taught to believe in their religions as well.

From an early age, I was taught that God always knew what was in my heart. Even *thinking* a bad thought was a sin, and I would be punished for all of those sins when I died. But how is it that I could be brought up in a loving household with people who still sinned so often? My sister was jealous of me; my brother would lie about whether he ate his vegetables; my mother would get angry and yell at us; my friends would lie and judge each other. I was a "good girl," yet I often got angry at my parents or hid things from them. I felt emotions such as selfishness, greed, even self-righteousness. Of course, this was attributed to the fact that we were "born in sin" and that sinful nature was attributed to Satan (aka the Devil). But if God was so powerful, how could He allow the Devil to have so much power in the first place? And did He have to wait 2000+ years after the fall of Adam and Eve to do something about it (namely, bring Jesus to come to save us from our sins)? What about all the people who were born and died before then? And why is sin still such a problem, even for those who have been "saved"?

It didn't help that at many of the churches we attended, we were judged for doing… or *not* doing… things that were okay according to the teachings in *another* church…or even one of the same denomination. And if the Bible was the only "divine" work of God, how come there were so many denominations in the first place?

I was once told by one youth group that I was "evil" because I went to movies, even if they were PG or G rated, while the other churches we attended never mentioned movie-going as a sin (other than not seeing rated R movies, of course). My mother was actually kicked out of one church for speaking in tongues, as that was "the devil's speech", while it was praised in another church one town over (ironically, both of them were Baptist churches) as a gift from God. Some churches believed in "gifts of the spirit" while others swore that these very same attributes were the "mark of the devil."

If these were all Christian churches, why did they disagree on so many things?

Then there was Catholicism, which most of my friends were brought up to follow. Catholicism is also a Christian religion, but their rules are vastly different from those of Protestants… they even read a different Bible. For one, they had to kneel a lot. And go to confession. And catechism. And then there was

Lent, which they took very seriously. And the rosary. And Protestants weren't allowed to even attend Catholic services. And whoa be to anyone who fell in love with someone who wasn't also Catholic; how would they possibly bring up their children? Many Catholic churches wouldn't allow their members to attend a Protestant church, even if it was just to go to a wedding or to Vacation Bible school.

With all these contradictions and questions running around in my head, I decided to do what any avid reader would do – I picked up the Bible and started to read it myself. So in the 6th grade, I got myself a Living Bible (because being able to check off each chapter as I went was really cool) and I began read one chapter a day, starting with Genesis.

But that only gave me *more* questions; questions that couldn't be answered by any minister, at least not to my satisfaction. Questions like "How fair is it for God to punish all of humanity – for eternity, no less – for the decision of one woman (Eve), who ate from the Tree of Life?" "If Adam and Eve were the first humans that God created, after Cain slew Abel, and he was condemned to roam the earth alone, without being allowed to be helped by anyone… where did all those people in those other cities come from?" And how about "How can dinosaurs be real if the Bible doesn't mention them?" Or the bigger questions like, "'If God so loved the world' how come He's okay with condemning us to Hell for eternity?" Or "How come some of the most beautiful spirits I've ever met didn't go to church… or weren't even Christians?" Or "How is it that God spoke directly to so many people in the Old Testament, but He doesn't talk to us directly anymore?" Or "If Jesus is the only way to heaven, how is it there was so many other religions that say otherwise?" Or "How come it wasn't a sin to have many wives in the Old Testament but now it *is* a sin?" And one of my biggest questions, since I grew up in a Catholic town, was "How can it be a sin to eat meat on Friday, but the rest of the week it *isn't* a sin?"

Still, I knew that there was a "God" of some sort out there, and I spent a lot of time praying to Him, hoping that asking for forgiveness for my impure thoughts was enough to save me in the end.

From the start I was taught that God was a both a loving God and a God to be feared, and that never quite set right with me. We were supposed to love God… but it seemed that that love was given mostly out of fear… and if we did not show our love for God by going to church every week, or praying every night, or being baptized, it wouldn't matter how many good deeds we did… we'd still ultimately end up in Hell instead of going to Heaven. How could we love a God that could smite us at any time for making a mistake (aka a "sin")? What if we didn't even know something was a sin in the first place? Personally, I don't even *respect* someone that I fear; the emotion I feel about someone like that is closer to hate than love.

For me, proof in the existence of God came to me when I was 12 years old and my mother got ill. Her ovaries had burst, and she was bleeding internally. I still remember holding my mother's hand while she lay in bed, her skin deathly white… it was as cold as ice. Needless to say, I was terrified.

Ironically, the church we had been attending at the time was one that had until recently been called a "dead" church… which basically meant that the minister was very old and membership was down. Just a few weeks before my mother got ill, the church had hired a new minister. My parents had invited him to dinner one night soon after he arrived. All I could think of was that he looked just like Grizzly Adams (from the TV show), full beard and all. Yet he seemed nice enough. And he preached that God was a *loving* God, while the last minister had preached that God was a *jealous* God; one to be feared. (I did not like *that* minister one bit.)

The night my mother lay dying, my father called the new minister, and he came right over to the house… and he brought the Elders of the church with him. Together, they sat around my mother in her bedroom and began to pray. That is when I remembered the verse in the Bible that stated "When two or more are gathered together in my name, I am there in their midst. (Matthew 18:20)." That was the first time in my life I acquainted a feeling of reverence when it came to God.

But nothing happened. She was still dying. Soon thereafter, she was taken by ambulance to the hospital.

Since I was too young, I couldn't go to the hospital with her; I had to stay home with my younger sister and brother.

The next day, I remember being told that my mother was in surgery again. I stood in the kitchen watching my father stare out the kitchen window. He stood like that, without moving, for what seemed like hours. It was then that I knew that my mother was not going to make it. So I prayed, "God, please don't take my mother. I am too young to be a mother." Instinctively I knew that my father would not survive if she were to die and I would be left to take care of my siblings.

My mother recovered, and a few days later, she came home from the hospital. She told us that the doctor had said it was a miracle; that it was nothing he had done, because she had simply lost too much blood… that there was no reason she should have survived. How often have you heard a doctor admit that science didn't have the answer?

Years later, my mother told me that she *had* died on the table that day in surgery…that she saw herself floating up above her body, and she'd watched the doctors while they worked on her. At that time she also had said a similar prayer to mine: "Please, God, I can't go yet, as my children will be left without parents." She also knew that my father wouldn't live without her, leaving us alone to fend for ourselves.

She made a full recovery.

That was when I experienced my first miracle.

And I learned about the power of prayer.

When I was a young, we had a neighbor across the street who was rumored to be a witch. That rumor was confirmed the day that the neighbor brought a man to our front door. When my mother opened the door, a warlock stood before her, dressed like... well, a warlock. He was entirely in black, with a dark cape and a tall, dark hat. The only thing that wasn't black was his white beard, though I don't think he was very old. He told my mother that he could tell she had the gift of ESP. Then he asked her if she wanted to join his coven. I remember my mother calmly declining his offer and slowly shutting the door. She told me never to speak of that again.

3
ALL WE NEED IS LOVE

I am human and I need to be loved
just like everybody else does.
LUCY

When I was in the 10th grade, my mom and dad decided to become foster parents. Our first experience was with a 15 year-old girl. She was to share a room with me. She came from the big city and had kinky, curly black hair. She smoked, listened to heavy metal music all night (via headphones), and she let us know that she had no idea who her father was. She was also sexually active, a fact that she displayed almost immediately by donning a red negligée and parading around the house in it… until my mother made her change before my father could see her. She was also good at running away. And she was very good at lying. I had never met anyone quite like her. She fascinated me the same way a car wreck on the highway would. Within the first week she had run away from the house at least twice.

Needless to say, she didn't last long in our house.

After that, my parents made a few other attempts with teenagers, but soon they decided that it was easier to take in smaller children and mold them into becoming better people, rather than start with kids who already had their personalities set.

But taking in babies was no picnic either. Having a baby is hard enough in the best of circumstances, but add drug addictions, a history of physical and/or mental abuse, neglect, and malnutrition to the mix, and those children needed a lot of extra love and attention.

It was then I learned two important lessons. For starters, I saw first-hand what the lack of love did to a person, especially in one so young. They say the first 3 years are crucial to the mental and physical health of a child, and now I know why. If a child is not held, nurtured or loved enough during those first few years, he or she can grow up to believe that the world is a harsh, ugly place… and treat others accordingly. And they rarely love themselves, which makes it that much harder for them to love others.

And because so many children do not feel loved when they are little, they grow up to become parents who abuse and/or neglect their *own* children, perpetuating an ugly cycle. They do that because they know of no other way to be.

The most significant example of how love effects a child came from the babies my parents took in who had the HIV virus. At the time, AIDs was still very new to us, and extremely terrifying. My parents had to take a special class to learn how to take care of these children; how to make sure that no blood came into contact with any open wounds, whether from a cut or even in their stool. These poor children had to take a lot of medications… as well as visit the hospital at least once a month for their first 2 years to get these huge injections, with needles inserted into their necks… needles that were almost as long as they were.

When I got older and had my own children, I would go to the hospital with my mother and take her foster children in to have their shots, because she couldn't handle watching the doctors insert those needle into their necks. Even though they weren't her children, she felt for them as if they were her own.

And every single child who came to our house with the HIV virus left without having it… which many did not know was even possible. Apparently, if a woman has HIV virus or even AIDs itself, she automatically passes the virus onto her child, but the child does not necessarily contract AIDs from that. They can become negative and end up living long, healthy lives.

I still remember my mother telling me that the social workers wanted my parents to take as many children with HIV as possible, because they had the "magic touch." And of course, that "magic touch" was LOVE. Those children were able to fight off a horrible, life-threatening virus because they knew they were loved. They simply had a reason to fight for their lives.

The second lesson I learned while watching my parents take in foster kids was what a huge responsibility it was to care for children… and I wanted no part of it. I had big dreams, you see. I was going to become an actress. Or make movies. Or at the very least, travel the world. And kids just didn't fit into that picture. I didn't want the responsibility. At that point, I didn't even know if I wanted to get married.

Ironically, I never felt neglected when my parents were taking care of these other children, though I distanced myself from them for the most part. They didn't seem to be part of my world. I was nearing the end of my high school career, and I was rarely home, so I didn't have to live with foster kids as much as most of my brothers and sisters did. For that, I am grateful.

As I look back on that time in my life, I still cannot fathom a person having a child and not being able to show it love, regardless of their personal circumstances. I had always figured that with so many organizations set up to care for children, a parent had no excuse to make sure that child was cared for, even if they couldn't be the ones to do it themselves. In my naiveté, I judged them for not being able to love their own children.

Today, I have 5 adopted sisters and brothers, with many others who aren't biologically or legally related that I still consider to be part of my family. Each one of them has taught me so many things about myself and my own capacity to love. And I wouldn't trade those experiences for the world.

That is how I learned that there is nothing you can't accomplish as long as you have love.

When I was in junior high, I had a horrible dream about a beach filled with people who were dying. It took me quite a while to shake that dream. But a few weeks later, while I was watching TV, I saw a preview for a new horror movie that was coming out in the summer. It was called Blood Beach. The images they showed were nearly identical to my dream! Yet I had never heard of this movie before. This was in the days before cell phones or computers, so there was no way for me to know about this movie until the preview was on TV. And I would have remembered if I had read about it. That that was when I knew I had inherited my mother's gift of ESP. But it frightened me so much that I rejected the gift (of what the Bible would call "prophecy"); I don't even know if I have it any more.

4

B+ Person

Who cares what other people think?
SALLY

All through elementary and high school I mostly got straight A's (math was always the one thorn in my side). I prided myself on making sure all of my homework was done right and on time. And with the exception of missing two weeks of school in the second grade when I had the chicken pox, I never missed a day. It never even crossed my mind to skip school when everyone else was doing it.

Even though I was in the Honor Society in high school, I never thought of myself as anything more than an average student…. Or average *person*, for that matter. Whenever my mother used to say "You're beautiful," I would tell her "You *have* to say that; you're my mother." And I honestly believed that I was not much to look at. My hair was not curly enough; my thighs were too big; my boobs weren't big enough. I wore glasses, so I looked like the nerd that I was. Basically, I was nothing special.

More than that, I seemed to be quite good at many things, yet I didn't excel in anything either. I was a decent daughter, only getting grounded once all through high school. I did my chores when I was told to, and conveniently forgot to when I wasn't told to. I didn't swear, steal or sleep around. I was a decent writer – getting a few small articles published in the local paper. I was a good swimmer, but I could not have rescued anyone successfully. I was part of the chorus in school, but was never asked to do a solo. I was never called ugly or fat, though I was never happy with my body. I had a few good friends, but I wasn't what people would consider "popular". I knew I was a bit of a nerd, though I don't remember anyone ever calling me that to my face. My teachers liked me well enough, though I was never a teacher's pet. I didn't start dating until my junior year of high school, though that might have been as much a product of living in such a small town as anything else. I never got fired from a job; nor did I get promoted. I have my name on the back of a record album of "the best singers in the state" when I was in the 11th grade. But of course so did 200 others kids. I got any job I applied for, in the days when getting a job was as easy as showing up for it. I got into the private college I wanted to attend because I took the required classes (and had the grades)... and I received my Bachelor's Degree in the required 4 years, but my grades were average. I didn't have to try too hard to get anything I wanted, so I had few real successes... but even fewer failures.

I am a decent wife, and a good mother, though I doubt I would win any awards in either category. I have an eye for photography and I am a slightly above-average editor (after 15 years of experience, I wrote a book on the subject). And I have managed to keep my own business afloat for more than 17 years to date, though I am still just a sole proprietor and have no employees under me.

Don't get me wrong: I am not complaining about being a B+ person. It has kept me humble. And I never really had dreams of conquering the world, or even of becoming a CEO of some big company. Though I would like to excel in just one thing; to be known for accomplishing something extraordinary... as I'm sure Charlie Brown would as well. Then again, I have interests in so many areas that I find it hard to stick to one long enough to become the "best" at it.

In this game called life, perhaps what we are all really meant to excel in is our personal spiritual journeys. That is, after all, why we are here, don't you think? Otherwise, what is all this running around really about? We live, laugh, cry, love, hate and eventually die, but to what end? Hence, my continued interest in my own personal spiritual journey.

When I was in high school, I had a major crush on a guy whose mother was my own mother's best friend. He was 2 years older than me. It was obvious that he knew I liked him, and he flaunted that fact whenever I was around. For my 16th birthday, my parents gave me a birthday party at a roller skating rink in the city… and my mother invited him to come to my party. I was ecstatic… until he showed up with his <u>girlfriend</u>.

For my junior prom, I went with a friend of mine. We had a nice enough time. Since neither one of us had a car, we had to get a ride home with the photographer, who was also my neighbor. The most memorable part of the entire evening was being stuffed into the back seat of his car, along with a ton of photography equipment (we were literally sitting on some of it). I vowed not to go to my senior prom unless my date actually owned a car.

5
BORN AGAIN

When I was 12, my parents became "born again." We had always considered ourselves Christians, of course, though that basically meant we said a prayer of thanks before meals and we celebrated Christmas and Easter with all the usual aplomb. But when my parents became "born again", our lives began to change.

Naturally, we started to attend church more regularly, though not as often as you might think, since my parents seemed to find it rather difficult to settle on a particular church. They all had so many different rules to follow, after all. So we had to find the right fit.

We had left the "dead" church after my mother recovered from her surgery, even though we were all grateful for their prayers (which I now know worked quite well). For a while we attended a Baptist church the next town over, but my mother decided she didn't like that one because they frowned on her for speaking in tongues*. Eventually, we found a church two towns over that was cool, because they had a band that would play Egyptian music before each service. But that church fired its minister because his oldest son got into some kind of trouble with the police (don't forget the adage that "For if a man cannot manage his own household, how can he take care of God's church?" (1 Tim 3:5). We also tried an Episcopalian and Methodist church, but my parents seemed to prefer the Baptist ones.

My various experiences at so many Protestant churches of different denominations gave me a first-hand look at hypocrisy…. And what it felt like to be judged. Never have I felt as judged as I did whenever I stepped into a new church. Even at such a young age, it wasn't hard to tell that the people there were comparing themselves to one another to see who best measured up to their version of what God wants us to be. You know people are looking at you, thinking "What is it that she's wearing?" "I wonder what do they do for a living." "How much will they tithe?" Sadly, there was so much emphasis on what was on the *outside* that they didn't have time to take care of what was in the *inside*. At least I never left a church feeling very nourished spiritually. Most of the time, I found it hard to believe that God was even there with us during a service; that it was all just for show. We were all there to put in our time, simply because the Bible said that we should go to church.

The differences in the religion my family practiced were even more pronounced when I was around my friends. Since I lived in a predominantly Polish Catholic town, I was the only one who didn't attend Catechism, or follow Lent, or listen to the Pope…which meant I could eat meat on Fridays (though I still haven't figured out if that meant I was sinning or not sinning).

For me, the hardest part was trying to having a birthday party during Lent. I had 3 girlfriends all though high school, and they each gave up the same thing every year: one gave up chocolate, another dessert, and the other cake, of all things. Which meant that for my birthday I had to have vanilla cupcakes for *dinner* or no one would be able to eat with me. One year I begged my friends to give up something else just one time for me. They all refused. And yet these were the same girls who would also lie, gossip and otherwise "sin" the rest of the year, like everyone else. So what good did abstaining for a few weeks from something you enjoyed actually do for one's soul?

Still, I did manage to have a few spiritual moments during the years I attended church. Most of them occurred during the singing portion of the service, as it was then that people would let their guard down and pour their hearts out to God. Often I would find myself in tears as I listened (though I rarely sang along), and I wondered why. My mother once said that it was because I was being "cleansed" of all the negativity within me.

And though I believe that was a nice enough sentiment, now I tend to believe that it was more likely that I could feel the people's pain, sorrow and loneliness… their need to feel as if they belonged… their plea for God to give them solace when they, too, were not feeling as if God was listening.

Needless to say, I didn't attend church often. And when I did, I spent most of my time looking at the clock, waiting for it to be time to go home.

Still, as the dutiful daughter I was, I eventually got baptized in a lake in a beautiful ceremony, though I didn't feel any different on the inside after I did it. I couldn't help the questions that kept coming up when I'd attend Sunday School. Questions like, "How does a loving God kill so many people?" "What does the shedding of blood have to do with making your soul clean?" "How come all of God's faithful were tested in such horrible ways – such as prison, or being swallowed by a whale, or asked to kill your own son?" "Why was it acceptable for men to marry multiple women in the Old Testament and now sleeping with more than one person is a sin?"

Yet I didn't feel as if I could ask the questions that were teeming around inside of me, because when I did I would be looked down on, get scolded, or get too many different answers. So I held them in and tried to be as good a person as I could be because God said I had to… or else. I mean, look what happened to Eve… she got kicked out of the Garden of Eden for eating an apple. If it was so important for them not to eat the fruit of that tree, why did God put it there in the first place?. And what about Moses, who was never allowed to see the Promised Land because of one mistake, even though he had obeyed God for more than 40 years? What about when God destroyed an entire city (Sodom & Gomorrah) or turned Lot's wife into salt just for turning around when fire reigned down behind her, killing everyone she ever knew? Or when He let Moses kill hundreds (if not thousands) of soldiers in the Red Sea? Or when God destroyed the entire world in a flood? What more would He do to little old me for not being able to follow the Ten Commandments?

I spent the next 8 years of my school education feeling as if I didn't fit in, much like everyone else. I went to school dances, and participated in school plays. I was in the chorus and on the Yearbook Committee. I had the occasional school-boy crush. I went to my Junior and Senior proms. I spent my weekends going to the mall or the movies with my girlfriends. In the eleventh grade I got a job and had a boyfriend. Life was good, right?

So why did I find myself seeking out those who I knew didn't believe as I did, so I could get their take on how they felt about God, sin and all of that? Sure, a part of me figured that God told us to "witness" to others, as that would get us "crowns in heaven", but I did it more to find answers to my own unending questions regarding the contradictions I was finding in the Bible… along with what adults were telling me about God, Heaven, sin and the like.

Looking back now, I see that I was making my first steps down the road of my personal spiritual journey. Becoming "born again" was just a stage I had to go through to get me started.

* *"Speaking in tongues" is something can happen when someone becomes "born again" or spirit-filled. It is mentioned in the Protestant Bible 35 times. It is often referred to as a "heavenly language" though some churches believe it is from the devil. Hence, the controversy.*

Once I was driving to the mall with my sister. We were on the highway and my car ran out of gas... at the top of hill. At the bottom of the hill was a gas station. So I put the car in neutral and rolled down until I was in front of the gas pump. "Fill 'er up!" I said with a smile. You should have seen the expression on the gas attendant's face.

One of my co-workers asked me out to a movie my senior year. He took me to a drive-in. He had a really big car (don't ask me what make or model). After the first movie was over, he asked me if I was going to "sit way over there all night". I told him it was much cooler by the open window. "Fine!" he said. It was then I realized what he had planned for the evening... but I simply was not interested. Luckily, he respected my wishes. Unfortunately, when I got home, I guess my parents hadn't expected us to stay for the double feature; I got grounded for staying out past curfew.

6
THE RED ROAD

When I was in the seventh grade, my family made a trip to Oklahoma to visit my aunt and uncle and 3 cousins, who lived on one of the Army bases there. That was my first introduction to real Native Americans. My cousins would play with this group of boys who were Crow, Choctaw and Cherokee. I was enthralled with their long black hair, dark skin, and of course, their accents. They seemed both foreign and yet somehow more "real" than anyone I had ever known.

When I got home, I began to study everything I could about Native American culture, including their spiritual beliefs. This journey down the Red Road opened my eyes to a whole new way of looking at the world. It seemed to me that those who still followed the "old ways" were more connected to nature and their own soul's journey than Christians were. Their myths and legends were put into place to teach their children the value of family, respect for all things, and connectedness to all. These were all very new concepts for me, and I found myself enthralled by it all. I wasn't sure if I believed that there were such things as shape-shifters or that a shaman could really heal a person simply by cleansing one with sage and saying a few specific words… but how much different was that then praying over someone who was dying in *my* religion?

Native Americans believed that if you harvested a crop, that you were to leave a portion unpicked, so that those plants could regrow again in the next season… to care for Mother Earth. When they would kill an animal for food, they would honor that animal's spirit, thanking it for giving its life so that they may live… and then they would use every bit of that animal, leaving nothing to waste. They honored each other in all ways. Everyone who lived in their tribe was a "relative" even if not biologically, and they were treated accordingly. Each tribe had a chief, but big decisions were made by the elected group as a whole. Sex was a natural part of life and not something to be ashamed of. They respected their elders. The entire village would care for all of the children; everyone in the tribe was part of their family. And those who were handicapped in some way were revered for being "special" instead of hidden away from others. Plus, they respected others who believed differently from them.

Amazing! I couldn't help but think that this was the way I wouldn't mind living. These people cared for the earth and all the creatures on it... at least until the white man shoved them into secular schools, taught them English and forbid them to worship the way they had been doing for generations. Were these same people going to Hell simply because they didn't follow the God in the Bible? How did that make sense?

This is when I began to really question my place in the world...and what part religion should actually take in my life.

Not soon after I graduated from high school, then I finally got a chance to go on a date with my high school crush. He took me out to dinner and drinks… quite a few drinks… afterwards. When we got back to his parents' house, where I was staying the night (since he lived in a different state), he finally kissed me. Then he passed out. To this day, I still don't know if he remembers that kiss. And we never did go on a second date.

The day I came back from that visit/date, my mother told me that my boyfriend had called while I was gone… and she actually told him that I was out with another man, and that I had stayed the night! She never would've done such a thing if she didn't dislike my boyfriend as much as she did. Anyone who knows my mother never would've believed she'd do such a thing.

7
TALKING HEADS

My grandmother on my mother's side was schizophrenic. Because of that, she had to live in a mental hospital on a military base (she had been a nurse in the Army). That was one of the scariest places I have ever been in my life. I still shiver a bit when I think of it today. I dreaded visiting my grandmother there. My parents and I would go into the facility to take her out for the day and there would be old men and women walking about the place, many of them with missing limbs, most of them in various stages of undress, all of them mumbling to themselves. When I looked into their eyes, they seemed to be dead inside. None of them would speak to us, or to each other. A few would even openly pee in the hallways. And don't get me started on the *smell*! Even at such a young age, I knew that this was where these people had been placed while their families waited for them to die. Not a very honorable way to care for our soldiers, I can tell you that. (Though I am ashamed to say I am glad that my grandmother didn't have to live with us.)

Whenever my grandmother would spend the night with us – which wasn't often, thank God – she would sit in one of the recliners in our living room and smoke, often with one lit cigarette in each hand. She would usually forget to wear her teeth (dentures), which always grossed me out. Sometimes she would even forget to wear underwear, which is quite awkward, considering she only wore skirts. I have to admit, I was a bit afraid of her. But she was my grandmother, so we were taught to treat her with respect.

At night she would wander around our house, as she found it difficult to sleep. I will never forget the sound of her cough; it seemed she was hacking up an entire lung. I vowed I would never smoke after hearing that cough, and I never have.

For the most part, she seemed sane enough when she would visit us. She always told me "Listen to your mother" while at the same time scolding my mother for not listening to *her*.

As I got older, my grandmother would tell me about the "voices" that would speak to her. These voices would often tell her to do things that she didn't really want to do, but she would have to obey them (she didn't say why). She tried to explain to me that she had stabbed a man because "Satan told me to"; that was why she was put in the military hospital.

It seems that for some reason my grandmother had an affinity for me – perhaps because I was her first grandchild. But because of this, whenever she would stay the night, I would have horrible nightmares. But these would feel like much more than just nightmares – they seemed to be REAL. In these nightmares, I would be in this room that was entirely black, and these huge talking heads – I had assumed they were human, but thinking back on it, I cannot be sure of that – would be floating high up above and around me. They would all be speaking to me, sometimes as one, and not always in English. And as they would speak, their voices would get louder and louder, and they would speak faster and faster. It didn't matter if I covered my ears; the sound would not get any dimmer. It was more than a little terrifying.

Years later, my mother told me that my father had had the exact same type of dreams whenever my grandmother was in the house with us. This verified my belief that somehow we had been seeing actual beings from another realm... perhaps demons of some sort... though to this day I still have no idea what they wanted from me. All I do know is that when I could remember to say out loud, "Get thee behind me, Satan!" the heads would disappear and I would wake up.

That was my first experience with evil.

The day I arrived at my college dorm for the first time, I was anxious to find out who my roommates would be. When my parents and I walked into the dorm, I realized I was the first to arrive, so I chose my bed by putting my luggage on it and then I went to sign up for classes. When we came back a few hours later, one of the other beds had been made, but there was no sign of my roommate. So we went down to check out the bonfire they were having for the new arrivals. When I got back, the last bed had been made, but still no sign of either roommate. I began to wonder if my roommates were ghosts. A few hours later, after I said goodbye to my parents, they finally showed up.

I had been dating my first boyfriend for a year by the time I started college. He was going to college a few states over from me. Eventually, I met a guy at school and we became sort of a couple (though we didn't officially "date", since we were both stuck on campus). During the second semester, my boyfriend told me that I wasn't much fun...which means I wouldn't drink with him and I didn't like to party. On the same day, the guy I was seeing at school told me I made him think "impure thoughts" and that I was corrupting him – we did, after all, attend a private Christian college. So I wasn't good enough for one guy, and I wasn't bad enough for the other. For one whole afternoon I contemplated suicide.

8
THE BIBLE

Whenever it's one man against an
institution, there is always a tendency
for the institution to win!
CHARLIE BROWN

One day in 7th grade English, my teacher asked the class if anyone had ever read the entire Bible from front to back. When I raised my hand, he was shocked; he told me that I was the first person in his 30 years of teaching who had actually done it.

I believe reading the Bible is what jump-started me on my spiritual journey. Up until then, I had always relied on what others had told me regarding what the Bible was saying. Of course, I had often read *passages* in the Bible, following along as the pastor would read during a sermon, but after a few versus, he would inevitably spend the next hour explaining what those ten passages meant.

But as I read, especially once I got to the New Testament, I began to see inconsistencies between what the preachers were teaching about God and what the Bible's message seemed to be conveying. Mainly, what it seemed to come down to was interpretation; what each passage meant depended on who was reading it and the lesson they were trying to teach. For example, how many times have we been told to "turn the other cheek" when someone did something bad to us? [Matt. 5:39] This is supposed to be a lesson in loving your enemies. But then I read Proverbs 20:22, where we're taught that God will "avenge" anyone who does us wrong. So which is it – do we love our enemies or wait for God to smite them? If that's so, that doesn't seem to be very loving.

This is where I began to think more about the concept of Hell. One of the things that bothered me the most was the fact that the Bible says that we can go to Hell regardless of the kind of sin that has been committed; meaning that if I lie to my parents, I will get the same punishment as someone who committed murder, even someone as evil as Hitler. In the same token, that very same murderer can wait until he is about to be given a lethal injection on Death Row before asking God for forgiveness and he can go to Heaven… but if I get hit by a car before I ask for forgiveness for lying, I will be sent to Hell. How does that make sense?

I think the hardest thing for me to fathom was how an all-powerful Creator of the universe could allow this fallen angel (Satan) to create a place of fire and brimstone in the first place, never mind send his children – His creations – whom He loves, to spend eternity there when we do something… well… human. And what about the fact that for a few thousand years, the only way to avoid going to hell was to shed the blood of animals… and then the blood of his "only begotten son"? If God is the one who makes the rules, these rules don't seem to make a hec of a lot of sense. Why does forgiveness have to depend on the shedding of blood anyway?

I once dated this guy who believed that "God is a concept for the poor, to give them something to hope for, so they won't fall into despair." At the time, I thought that was ridiculous, but of course I was still a "believer" and nothing was going to persuade me otherwise. It seemed that even then, when part of me was searching, I still had my blinders on pretty tight.

Though it does stand to reason why he believed that way, if you think about it. I mean, when my life was easy and money wasn't an issue, I didn't think too much about God. Sure, I was curious about the messages I was receiving in church, but I managed to find any number of ways to easily justify my actions to fit what I was told God wanted me to do. As long as I went to church on Sundays and prayed before mealtimes (most of the time), and "tried my best" to be good, asking forgiveness for past transgressions as often as possible, that's all that was expected of me… from a spiritual standpoint. But when something bad would happen, or money began to become an issue in my life, God was suddenly brought to the forefront.

And of course, when that happens, we all say "God, where have you been?" as if it's God's fault that we had been too busy to pay Him any mind up until then. And this seems to be the way it is for most people, don't you agree? Life tends to get in the way of our spirituality. God only becomes important when we feel as if our lives are out of control and we suddenly need Him.

This is where I began to learn more about judgment and hypocrisy.

It also explains a lot about why my life was so messed up once I graduated from college.

When my first husband proposed to me, he took me out on the town. He tried to get me into a horse and buggy, but I refused to go, stating that it was too expensive. When he put the ring on the table in front of me in the restaurant, I didn't notice it, though everyone else in the restaurant did. When he was about to ask me to marry him, I said, "Wait. This is all wrong. Please try again another time." (A few weeks later, he did.)

When I got married to my first husband, we had the wedding in my parents' back yard. My mother had bought my wedding dress for $50 (I wasn't there when she bought it). She also made a string of flowers for my head... as well as the wedding cake. My father made a small trellis that we got married under. One of my uncles was the photographer; my mother sang during the wedding; my best friend did my hair and makeup; my other uncle and cousins decorated my car with tin cans. I told my maid of honor and my 3 bridesmaids to "wear something nice"... and my bridesmaids each came in a different shade of pink, my maid of honor in a brighter shade, as if they had coordinated it... and they hadn't. All in all, the wedding only cost a few hundred dollars.

9
WE'RE *NOT* IN THE ARMY NOW

"It's amazing how stupid you can be
when you're in love."
LUCY

I met my first husband in a bar, strangely enough. If you knew me, you'd understand how strange a statement that was. I had just spent the last 3 years in a private Christian college, so going to bars was something I just did not do. Nor was I much of a drinker – even though, ironically, my first boyfriend had been an alcoholic. It was the summer between my junior and senior year when my girlfriend and I decided to give this bar a town over a try.

I had had one disastrous relationship that summer with a guy I had met at the bar, so this was to be our last visit before we both had to go back to college in our respective states. Near the end of the evening, this guy came over to where we were sitting and said to me, "You don't look like you belong here."

That was the smartest thing he could have said to me, as I did not feel as if I did (Who wants to look like they belong in a bar, after all?). That was the start of our relationship.

That man became my best friend from then on; we did everything together. He courted me through my last year of college, then he proposed. A month after I graduated, we were married. And a few months after that, we moved to Florida to work at Disney World. We thought we'd be living the American dream. But I was so not ready for the real world.

In less than a year, we had to file bankruptcy. Working for Disney wasn't as easy – or as financially advantageous – as we had thought it would be. Nor was it as much fun.

I tried a few other jobs – a collection secretary, a hotel clerk, a night auditor – but I just wasn't happy. It wasn't my marriage that was the problem, though my husband's inability to manage money certainly didn't help. Truth be told, both of us were very immature and naïve regarding our finances.

My dream had always been to make movies (it was what I went to college for), so I figured this would be a good time for us to make the move to California. Only, every time we started to make plans to move, our car would become totaled – though luckily neither of us ever got hurt. We had 3 cars in the three years we lived in Florida. To me, I took this as a sign from God that I was not meant to live in LA. Especially since the moment I mentioned moving back to my home state, within 3 days, everything had fallen into place and we were moving back East instead.

For the first few weeks we lived with my in-laws; I don't think I have to tell you how much fun that was.

Then I came up with the brilliant idea to join the Army. The plan was for me to enlist as a photographer. That way my husband and I could travel the world on Uncle Sam's dime, and I could get a degree in photography, which would only help me get closer to my dream of becoming a cinematographer.

So I proceeded with the steps it took to enlist. First, I had to get into shape… which meant losing about 30 pounds. There was a lot of work to be done. Still, we tackled it head-on, spending at least 4 hours a day exercising in one form or another (walking, biking, running, or spending the morning at Bally's), using Slim-Fast shakes as a substitute for 2 out of 3 of our meals, and exercising some more. It was grueling, and I was always hungry, but I was determined to stick with it.

A few months later, I still hadn't made my goal weight; actually, I had only lost 2 pounds. Though of course my husband had reached his goal within the first month.

Eventually, after much struggle, I finally reached my goal weight, and the date was set for me to enlist. That was when my husband informed me that he was going to enlist along with me – until that point, he had only lost the weight to be supportive of me. That hadn't been the original plan, but in theory it sounded good. Our recruiter explained that the Army tried very hard to keep married couples together. So off we went to enlist!

When it was all over, I had not passed the physical – due to some small technicality. (In those days, it was much harder to enlist in the Armed Forces, as they were actually trying to get people *out* of the Army.) But my husband *did* get in. That should have been good news... only he informed me that he was going to become an EMT and that we were going to live in Germany for the next 3 years. And all without first discussing any of this with me!

Needless to say, I was in shock. And within the next few days, he was off to Basic training.

By this time, I had moved back into my parents' house. I got a temporary night job and began the wait for my husband to graduate Basic.

That is when I met the love of my life... and my entire life was turned upside down. Suddenly, I was lying to my parents – and my husband – about where I had been every night, as we'd often skip work just to spend time together. I even had my sister-in-law cover for me once (she was not happy about lying to her brother-in-law!).

I couldn't understand what was happening to me. I had been brought up in a Christian household, with good values. I had only slept with one other guy before I'd met my husband, and after we were married I never once thought about sleeping with another man. Yet here I was having an affair, purposely lying to everyone I cared about to do so.... And it didn't feel *wrong*. How could that be?

Even worse, when I took the trip to the Army base in Texas to see my husband graduate from Basic training, I took this man along with me. To this day, I cannot explain why I did that, other than he asked if he could tag along.

The day I finally got to see my husband again was surreal. He had changed so much that I hardly recognized him; I actually had to check the wedding ring on his finger to make sure it was him.

His personality had changed as well. Now he was full of self-confidence. Truth be told, he was even a bit arrogant. He wasn't exactly rude or mean to me, but he was definitely not the same man I had married.

At least that is what I told myself when I realized that I was no longer in love with him. So that night, after he left my motel room, I wrote him a "Dear John" letter and sent it to him at the barracks to discover after I had left.

Needless to say, he didn't take that very well. The next day, while I was on the road, I received a phone call from the Army psychologist, who said that my husband had tried to go AWOL, and that he was threatening suicide if I didn't come to see him.

But instead of feeling compassionate and afraid for his life, I felt as if I was being manipulated; guilted into staying with him. Still, I drove back to Texas to see the psychologist so we could talk things out.

The psychologist said this problem between us wasn't as uncommon as one might think. And the Army would be willing to set us up in on-base housing for a few months – free of charge – while we went through marriage counseling. My husband wouldn't be shipped to Germany until our marriage was back on track.

That was a major crossroads for me. Do I stay and try to make my marriage work… especially since my husband hadn't done anything wrong… or do I run off with the new man in my life?

It didn't seem to be a hard decision. It only took me a few minutes to make up my mind. I told my husband good-bye and wished him luck in his life. For me, my marriage was effectively over.

To this day, I still cannot say what had happened to me to make me do things that were so against what I thought was my true nature. But love makes you do strange things.

I am happy to say that I have not regretted that decision, even if I did regret the way that I handled the situation.

It's lucky for me that I did leave my husband after all... because I was pregnant. And the baby wasn't his.

When I got married to my second husband, my fifth grade teacher (he was my all-time favorite teacher), was also a Justice of the Peace. That wedding cost even less than the first one. (Our 2 sons were also in attendance.)

After I met my second husband, we had a baby together, then we moved into an apartment, then we broke up, got back together, had another baby, and then we got married. A few months after that, we actually went on our first date.

My second husband was my "lawyer" in the divorce with my first husband. The entire divorce decree is actually hand-written by him.

10
HOMELESSNESS

It's a mistake to try to avoid the
unpleasant things in life…
but I'm beginning to consider it.
CHARLIE BROWN

Since I was in the second grade, I had considered my family to be well off. After all, we lived in a big house in a nice neighborhood (where we never saw one homeless person). I always had new clothes for the first day of school. We never lacked for anything. My siblings and I went on every field trip our schools offered. My sister and brother also got to go to college – we were the first in my entire family to do so. Each of us even got to spend at least a month in another country during college – thanks to my parents. Every summer we would go on vacation to the beach for at least 2 weeks. And the Christmas tree was always full-to-overflowing with gifts. We weren't exactly middle-class, but that didn't matter to me.

So when I found myself homeless, it was more than a little of a shock. And I am sorry to say I did not handle it very well.

At the time, I thought that this was my punishment from God for leaving my husband and getting pregnant by another man. Never mind that I was in love with this man. My parents thought I must have had a mental breakdown, or that the father of my child had tricked me somehow into running away with him… or worse, that he had gotten me pregnant against my will, and that he was continuing to abuse and brainwash me.

For over a year after I left my husband, I tormented myself with thoughts of guilt and remorse for "living in sin" while we struggled to find a way to survive. Worse than the fact that I was sinning by living with a man who was not my husband, I had betrayed my marriage vows and hurt my family in the process. I did not feel as if I had the right to find happiness with the man I loved, never mind get out of this financial hole we had dug for ourselves.

But looking back on that experience, I can see how that was the biggest wake-up call for me in terms of my spiritual journey. Ripped away from the safety and security of my husband and my family, I could finally see the world around me for what it really was. And I was realizing that this safety and security I had always felt were really just illusions. I mean, look how easy it was for me, an intelligent college graduate in her mid-20's, to become homeless.

The most surprising thing was that I found myself being helped by people I had previously considered to be the "unlovable" in God's eyes… people who I would have labeled "sinners" and who I would have avoided at all costs. My way of seeing the world – as if people were either "good" or "bad" – was quickly shattered as those I had considered to be "god-fearing people" turned me away and/or ignored my struggles, while people I barely knew would offer a helping hand for no reason other than the fact that they had a good heart…even when they didn't have much to give in the first place.

I will never forget this one woman we worked with who lived in a small, ramshackle house. When we learned there was no work for us that night – we were all working for the same temporary agency – she offered to let us stay in her house… and sleep in her bed… so that I didn't have to sleep in our van in the cold. And then there was the convict who was covered in tattoos, who would often give us a ride to work so we didn't have to spend the gas money. And this sweet Hungarian woman who would give us discounts on a motel room – or let us stay a few extra hours past check-out time – when she knew I needed the rest.

My eyes were really opened the day that we went to the Red Cross to ask for help. This middle class black woman told us that she couldn't help us, because we had "shelter" – namely, our van, and that we would have to leave. Never mind that we could not afford the gas to get us to a place to find food or work. Never mind that it was winter and freezing outside and we couldn't run the van at night to keep warm. Never mind that she was as pregnant as I was. To this day, I marvel at how that woman could sleep at night. (And I will never donate to the Red Cross because of it.)

The man I had fallen in love with had never gone to church a day in his life, yet he was working at temporary jobs for minimum wage, selling his blood almost every day so that he could buy me food! He would often go without eating for days to make sure me and the baby would get enough nutrition. How could this man be considered a "sinner" in God's eyes? And what about the others who would give us the shirt off their backs, for no reason other than we were fellow human beings who needed help?

It was during this time in the city that I began to wonder how these lower class people, most of whom had never stepped inside a church, could treat me with respect and compassion, while those who were members in long-standing of their local parishes could look upon me with disdain... if they even deemed me worthy of attention in the first place. It began to wonder how these non-Christians could embody the values that *Christians* were supposed to exhibit while regular church-goers could step right over me and go on their merry way without a second thought. It pained me to think that *I* may have been like this as well!

Even my own, loving, Christian parents had shown me their true colors when they refused to help me and my child because I had "sinned" by breaking my marriage vows. I shudder to think of the number of times I was in real danger while the two of us slept on the streets, never knowing where or when our next meal would come from. Of course, I know now that I was being looked over by my spirit guides, but then all I "knew" was that I was being punished for my sins, and how!

The main lesson I learned through this experience was not to judge people by their outward appearance... or even to judge them at all. It's impossible to tell why a person is in the circumstance he or she is in... and what right do we have to judge them anyway? When you are homeless in a big city where you don't know a single soul, you tend to meet people you would never otherwise meet growing up in a middle class town on the East Coast. I am not ashamed to admit that until I was homeless, I had been a bit of a snob. I am not proud of that fact, but I most definitely am not a snob any longer. I have no idea why I ever thought I was better than people who had less than me, but I did.

That was when I learned what true compassion really was.

The day I came home from the hospital after the birth of my first son, I called my husband to tell him he had to sign the paperwork that stated that he was not the father, since technically we were still married. He refused. So I told him I would mail him the child support order in a few days instead. He agreed to sign off that he wasn't the father after all.

Every child is told the story of their birth once they get old enough to understand. What I realized after the birth of my second son was how completely different each of their births was. My oldest son was born in a country hospital, in the early morning, via a vaginal birth. He was born with black hair and brown eyes and was circumcised. My youngest son was born in a city hospital, late at night, via C-section. He was born with blond hair and blue eyes and was not circumcised.

My youngest son was often sick, so it wasn't unusual to see us at the ER one night when he had another ear infection. But this time, I met a woman there who was also there with her daughter. It turns out we both had our children on the same night in the same hospital; it was she who was pacing up and down the hallway while I was in labor. We became fast friends; still are to this day.

11
I VOWED I WOULD NEVER HAVE CHILDREN

*"Each generation must be able to blame the previous
generation for its problems. It doesn't solve anything,
but it makes us all feel better."*
LUCY

Since my parents started taking in foster children, I quickly realized how much of a responsibility it was to have children – and I wanted to no part of it.

Of course, the Universe had other plans for me.

With the birth of my first child, I quickly learned what unconditional love was all about. This was the kind of love spoken about in the Bible… the kind of love that God is said to have for all His children.

That was when the stories I was brought up to believe about God started to make less and less sense to me. Here was a God who made us in His image, I was taught… the same as I had made (or "created") my son in my womb… and I loved him so much that sometimes my heart would ache, it was so full to bursting. Even before he could speak, there was this unbreakable bond between us.

To me, he was perfect.

I still remember the first time I had to say "no" to my son. It hurt me to do so, for my only wish was to give him everything he wanted and never see him hurt or sad. But of course, as a parent, we know we have to let our children learn and grow – while staying safe, if at all possible – and that means they have to do some things they don't want to do – or stop doing some things they want to. In order for a child to learn to walk first, he has to fall down, and learn how to pick himself back up. Still, since you can't carry him around for the rest of his life, you have to let him fall down and occasionally hurt himself or he won't learn how to walk on his own. And because I loved him,

I had to let him make his own mistakes. But when he did, I certainly didn't love him any less. It was all part of the process of growing up.

But the God I was taught to believe in did not love ME in this same way. That God actually had *conditions* to His love. And oh so many rules as well! And not just rules to keep us safe (like don't touch the stove because it's hot). Rules for how to pray, what to eat, when to kill (so that it wasn't considered a sin), who we can sleep with (or not sleep with), etc. And if we, His children, didn't follow all of those rules (ie: go to church on Sundays, don't eat meat on Fridays, don't lie, cheat, steal, etc.)… become baptized, and repent all of our sins before we died, regardless of how much good we did in the world, we would end up in Hell… a horrible, hot, evil place. And the kicker was, we'd have to be there *forever*. And I for one do not know any parent who loves his/her child who would send that child to everlasting damnation, no matter what that child did.

If God was such a loving God, why were we taught to fear Him? As parents, we don't want our children to behave because they are afraid of us – at least most of us don't. We teach them not to cross the street without looking first so they won't get hit by a car. We teach them not to go around hitting – or otherwise hurting – others because it's not good to hurt others, and the consequences could be quite severe. But most of us don't demand that they "worship" us because we are bigger and stronger and know more then they do… and we certainly don't ground them forever no matter what rule they break or how mad they might make us. And of course, we don't stop loving them either.

I began to wonder how we could be made in God's image, with the same ability to feel emotions like hate, anger, jealousy and greed that God often felt… and yet we are made to believe that much of our personality traits are "evil". I mean, this same God who has killed more people than anyone can count (according to the Bible) would condemn us to Hell for killing someone else, even if it was for the very same reasons (ie. jealousy, greed, hate and anger). How does that make sense?

This is when I seriously began to question why I was a Christian in the first place.

Many years after I got married to my second husband, we found out that we had met many times before; when I was in high school, he would often drive his truck through the drive-thru at the fast food restaurant where I worked, and he'd ask me to bring his food out to him (I always refused). I bumped into him a few times when I went roller skating in the city; he was always with a bunch of guys and I bumped into him a few times, since I didn't know how to stop myself using the skates. And again, we met when I waitressed at an Italian place the summer before I went away to college. I often waited on him on Wednesdays (buffet night). We didn't meet officially until I had been married to my first husband for over a year.

When my husband and I first met, he told me he had 3 other children from 2 previous marriages. When my first son was a few months old, I decided to contact my husband's first wife to see about getting her son together with mine; so they could get to know each other. Silly me had thought that it was important for the half-brothers to have a relationship. His ex-wife showed up on my doorstep with court papers for my husband; she was suing him for current – and back – child support.

12
DIVORCE

CHARLIE BROWN: *I thought love was
supposed to make you happy.*
LINUS: *Where'd you get that idea?*

Most young girls often dream of the day they will get married. Some even plan it down to the minutest detail. I was never really like that. I just assumed that one day I would marry, and then never gave it another thought.

But I certainly never dreamed that I would one day be *divorced*.

After my divorce, my mother asked me why I ever got married in the first place. She was so upset and sad… and yes, more than a little angry that I had left my husband. I know she felt as if she had "lost" me. It didn't matter who the man was that I had left my husband for. I didn't matter that I truly loved this man, nor that we had a child together. My mother was sad for me because she thought she had lost me to evil. Many years later, after she had passed, I read a letter she had sent me… and I realized that even after I had been remarried for years at that point, she was still angry with me for getting divorced.

For a very long time, I saw my second husband through my mother's eyes. I judged him according to how I knew *she* felt about him instead of listening to my own heart... the same heart that had fallen in love with this man – a man who was strong, compassionate, loyal and kind – in the first place.

That judgment almost cost me my marriage.

That is another lesson I learned about religion: how it can separate us from one another by giving us an excuse to judge each other.

It took me many years – and a lot of therapy – before I could forgive myself enough for leaving my first husband and give myself permission to love my second husband the way I had when we had first met. And I can never get those years back. The very fact that my husband stayed with me through all of that is a testament to his love for me. Even when I left him for 6 months, he did not abandon me or his son. I will forever be grateful for that.

When we did get back together, it wasn't long after that that my second son was born. That in itself was a lesson in how much character my husband has. For the doctor had informed us around the 22-week mark that the chance of us having a child with Down Syndrome was 80%. And though my husband said from the start that he would never abandon his child no matter what, how can you know what you will really do until you are actually faced with a situation?

And the fact is, our son *was* born with Down Syndrome. And when the doctor informed us that "You never have to see him again," (because where we lived it was quite normal for parents to put their special needs children directly into the system), my husband had to be held back from punching the doctor out. *How dare he suggest such a thing?* he said. I explained to my husband that the doctor was just giving us our options, but it warmed my heart to know that he fully accepted the responsibility of caring for his son, regardless of his handicap. Just another measure of his good character.

As my boys grew up, whenever I compared my feelings of love for my own children with that of God's love for us, I would become more confused... and disturbed. For my children would do things that I didn't approve of – even though they knew the rules – and I would have to discipline them... but not once did I wish for them to be damned! (And what would that accomplish anyway?) I had a hard time spending a few days away from them, never mind the thought of all of eternity! I simply could not reconcile a God who "so loved his children" that He could ever let us go to Hell, regardless of what we had done. If God was so all-powerful, why couldn't he prevent that from happening?

Of course, we are taught that that is why Jesus was sent down to earth. The whole basis of Christianity is that God sent his son to "save" us [John 3:16]. But first he had to die a horrible death to do so. And yet, even though we're taught that Jesus didn't really die… but rather rose again… that still wasn't enough to really save us, for we can still go to Hell if we commit a sin, no matter how big or small. And of course, since we are human, sinning is inevitable, as no one is perfect. So it's as if we can't win no matter what we do. And we're back to obeying God out of fear, if we are truly honest about it.

Still, as a parent, can you imagine allowing one of your children to die for the *rest* of your children? You would think that a God that was all-powerful could find another way to thwart the devil without having his innocent son die such a horrible death. Especially since we are all still going to continue sinning anyway.

My biggest problem with all of this is that even once we are "saved" by accepting Jesus into our hearts, that still doesn't guarantee that we will go to Heaven. We still have to be good and follow all of God's rules, or we could still risk going to Hell. What's up with that? The answer I am usually given is that of course we still sin – we are only human – but all we need to do from then on is ask for forgiveness. Is it just me, or was the only thing that changed after Jesus died the fact that we don't also have to sacrifice a goat (meaning shed blood) when asking for forgiveness? I mean, Jesus sacrificing himself on the cross should have been enough to wipe out any need for hell, don't you think?

Than you add the fact that all of my friends had been brought up to believe that you had to be both baptized and go to Confession to be cleansed of your sins or you'd risk eternal damnation. So which was it?

And I'm not even touching on the fact that there are thousands of other religions out there. How is it possible that if God loves ALL his children, that only *Christians* have the correct, divinely written text (aka the Bible)? Never mind that we still have to decide whether the King James Bible is the right one, or the Lutheran, the Mormon, or the Catholic Bible, since those followers can all consider themselves Christian. If we are all God's children, isn't it possible that God could inspire us in many different ways? And why do the Muslims and the Jews, with the Torah and Koran, believe their books are divinely written as well? Is it possible that ALL of them are divinely written?

Throughout the years I have studied many different religions. And the main thing that I have found is that nearly all of them started with the same basic premise: that love, kindness, compassion, etc., are what we should all be striving for. But somewhere along the way, those who started those religions wanted more power – more control over their followers – and those messages became distorted, even corrupted. After all, what may have started out as a divine message from God had to go through humans, who are way less than perfect. There are bound to be mistakes that are made in the interpretation (linguistically and otherwise) of these divine texts, depending on who is doing the interpreting and for what organization… and what agenda… they ultimately had in mind in order to control the people.

Whenever I would ask these questions of my fellow Christians, if they could not spout off a Bible verse to support their reasoning, their default reply would always be "You have to take it on faith." But there is only so much faith can justify, don't you think?

When my husband and I went to the courthouse after he was summoned by the court, the first thing the Child Support Agent said to my husband was "I am going to recommend that you go to jail." So I asked him, "What happens if he does?" The agent explained that while my husband was in jail, he would earn a few cents a day while on work detail, but that that money would go toward his back child support. When he got out, 2 years later, he would still owe child support – only now it would be more, since he wouldn't have made much while in prison. So I said to him, "So, what you're saying is, you are going to keep my husband away from his 2 youngest children, leaving them without a means of financial support, so we will have to go on welfare. And since he can't pay much in child support, his 2 ex-wives and 3 other children will also be put on welfare. My husband will get 3 square meals a day, plus a roof over his head, free medical care and visitation with his children. And when he gets out, he won't be able to find a job, because he will be a convict, which means you'll have to put him back into jail." The Child Support Agent looked at me and my husband for a few moments, thought about what I said, and then he let him go home with an order to pay support every week.

13
MEN OF GOD

"That's life... all the trues are false
and all the falses are true."
CHARLIE BROWN

Since my parents attended many different churches through the years, we have met many different types of minsters – or what I would call "men of God," though that is more what they'd call themselves then how I think of them. And while I have no problem admitting that no one is perfect, I believe that most people would agree that if you are a leader of people, integrity should be a major part of your job description. And when it comes to those who lead a church congregation, ethics – not to mention, morals – should be at the top of that list as well.

Unfortunately, that was not the case with most of "men of the cloth" that I have come into contact with, other than the young minister who prayed over my mother on the night she lay dying.

The second minister that was a big part of my family's life was the man who took over the "dying" church I grew up attending after the other minister went on to bigger and better things.

My father had dreamed of starting his own business for years, and when he unexpectedly lost his job of 12+ years as a printer, that minister persuaded my father to go into the printing business with him. He agreed to put up the money my father needed to convert our basement into a small printing press (sound-proofing it and everything), and my father went to work.

I'm not sure exactly how long it was before my father realized that he was not making money fast enough to make the minister happy. All that I do know is that in less than a year, the minister pulled out his money and my father had to close up shop. In the meantime, my parents began to fight over money, or the lack of thereof. That was the first and only time that my siblings and I thought they might actually get divorced.

Needless to say, the friendship with that minister ended on a sour note.

To this day, I can't help but think that my father would still be running his printing press today if he hadn't gone into business with a minister, whose only thought was how much money he was going to make off of my father's labor.

The third minister to come into our lives seemed at first to be a life-saver for my husband and I. When our boys were little, we had made the decision to move out of state, away from family. My mother had passed away not long before, which was when we learned that she was the glue holding our rather dysfunctional extended family together. And with my father grieving, effectively shutting all of his children out of his life, there was nothing to keep us there. Besides, this was a chance for us to actually live in a house, something we would never get to do if we had stayed in that state.

Unfortunately, the woman we had rented from was kind of crazy. We learned this when her ex-husband showed up at the house about a year after we moved in, asking who we were. Apparently, she had rented HIS house to us, as he had won it in the divorce. So without notice, after less than 2 years, we were told we had to move again.

At this time, I was working part-time at a fast food restaurant. I would speak to this elderly minister every morning when he would come in to buy coffee. And each morning, he would ask me how I was doing. So one day when he asked, I broke down, explaining that we were being kicked out of our home and had no place to go.

The minister told me he had a house that he had bought for his son when he got engaged… only now his son wasn't getting married after all. So he'd be willing to sell this house to us as a rent-to-own for a very low price. But there was a catch… it was a fixer-upper.

He wasn't kidding. When we moved in, after having spent the summer working on the house to make it livable, as in actually putting up walls... the house still didn't have all its electricity… or any plumbing. But we had made a deal with him; we'd fix up the house in lieu of a down payment, and we could use the church annex next door to shower and wash our dishes until we got the plumbing installed. We agreed on a monthly rent and we moved in.

But before we made our first month's payment, the minister reneged on our verbal agreement, stating that it cost more than he thought to insure the place, and he promptly increased our rent. Never mind that he still hadn't brought the paperwork for us to sign.

That meant that there were often times when we could not afford the rent. So the minister agreed to take the cost of the rent out in trade. Since my husband was a handyman, the minister had him doing work on his own home, as well as for other homes that he was in the process of flipping, in order for him to make himself *more* money.

This wasn't a bad arrangement in theory, but at the same time, whenever something would go wrong on the property – such as when the sewer system backed up – somehow *we* were the ones who ended up having to pay to get it fixed, when that was supposed to be his responsibility as our landlord.

Then we realized that the rental agreement we signed said nothing about it being a rent-to-own.

After the rental agreement expired, we somehow never got around to signing a new contract, most likely because the minister knew that we would be demanding he add both the rent-to-own portion of the agreement, plus the fact that he'd be responsible should something else go wrong with the maintenance of the house until it was actually in our name.

Meanwhile, my husband had to take time off of his work as a long distance truck driver to have carpel tunnel surgery on both of hands, since they were so bad that he could no longer feel his fingers (once he almost got a ticket when a DOR cop stopped him for a routine check and he actually couldn't let go of the wheel). So to save time, he elected to have the surgery done on both hands at the same time.

He was about to go back to work when the Twin Towers were struck in New York on September of 2011, and we were under threat of a terrorist attack. Because of this, he could not find work, since the government had put restrictions on trucks with hazardous materials being driven over state lines.

So my husband figured he would become a cop, something he had always dreamed of being. He began the paperwork and went through all the red tape required to be hired, including taking a physical. It took a few weeks, but eventually he was given a start date.

An hour before he was to report to work, headquarters called and he was told not to report in; the man wouldn't tell us why.

An hour after that, my husband's doctor called; could we come in to the office? Never a good sign.

That was when my husband found out that he had diabetes. Now not only was he off the police force before he even began, but no truck driving company would hire him until his sugar levels were stable for at least six months.

So my husband got work as an electrician's helper, something he had been trained to do in high school. Only after just a few weeks, his hands were becoming numb (neuropathy) due to the diabetes. So he had to quit.

Next, he found a job as a taxi driver. But his eyesight was being effected by the diabetes, so he was restricted to day-only driving, and he wasn't allowed to drive on the highway. Because of that, he was not earning very much money.

His last option was to drive a school bus. But that was only part-time. And every single job change meant less money was coming in.

It got so bad for a while that we couldn't afford to pay any of our rent in cash, and my husband couldn't work quickly enough to make it up in trade, especially with his physical limitations. And he was falling into a pretty deep depression. I knew it was time to take some drastic measures. I had to find work, as my home business had only just started to garner an income, but it wasn't near enough for us to live on.

After a lot of praying, and sending out countless resumes, I found us a job as Family Teachers. We would live in a house – paid for – and take care of foster children, something we had already been trained to do, and my husband enjoyed mentoring children. It seemed my prayers had finally been answered.

So I informed the minister that we'd be moving out. I gave him at least a month's notice, even though we didn't have a lease that we'd be breaking. We could have legally moved out without giving him any notice, but we felt we owed him that much. And though he hadn't as yet threatened to kick us out for lack of payment, I knew that day would soon be coming. Even so, he got really upset with us when he realized we were actually leaving, which tells me that he was getting a lot more out of our arrangement then we were. Besides, it always bothered me that yet another "man of the cloth" was so concerned about money – so much so that that was the main thing he talked about whenever we got together.

He never actually spoke to us again after we moved.

Ironically, our move brought us into the life of yet another minister and his wife. Once again, I thought they were an answer to my prayers. Out of all the applications I had sent out for Family Teaching, only one man had replied – a minister from the other end of the country. And he even agreed to meet us before we made the decision to move.

We met him and his wife at a local Cracker Barrel, and two hours later the decision had been made. We were going to become Family Teachers!

Two months later, we had sold nearly everything we owned – including our 2 cars – packed our bags and our cat, and we took a plane across the country to start our new lives.

From the start, it seemed that we were not living up to the minister and his wife's expectations. We were obviously not "holy" or "righteous" enough for them. And though we were willing to follow all of their rules, which included not watching any television shows or movies that had anything to do with magic (like Harry Potter, which was one of our family's favorite movie series), eating together for breakfast and every weekday lunch, and attending an outside church every Sunday morning as well as their own services every Sunday night, apparently that wasn't enough. I was starting to feel as if this was more of a cult than a Christian organization, but I was determined that we would stick to our agreement and do our jobs for at least the next year.

But instead of sitting us down and having a conversation about what was expected of us, the minister and his wife conspired against us behind our backs. And that is not just me being paranoid. We found out just how they felt about us two months into our training. As we were about to become certified as foster parents in that state, so we could actually begin the job we had moved there for, the minister told my husband and I to meet them at their home. Instead of a belated "welcome" party, like we were expecting, we were ambushed by him, his wife and the church council. Not only were we told that "things just weren't working out," but apparently the council had been watching us closely this entire time, without our knowledge. They knew that I had been on anti-depressants (though it didn't seem to matter that I was no longer taking them, and hadn't been since we arrived). They also knew that my oldest son didn't like much of the food they prepared (he had always been very picky). And they were upset that my youngest son had to be schooled in the next town over, due to the fact that he didn't speak and no one there knew sign language; they would have preferred that all the children attend the same, one-room classroom on the property taught by 3 teachers, who were also on the church council.

But the minister and the council didn't want to hear anything from us in our own defense; they had already made up their minds. They gave us just 7 days to move out, knowing we had sold or given away almost everything that we owned to get there. No matter that we didn't even own our own vehicle.

We had done nothing wrong; we had not broken any rules. But we were out.

Chalk up another instance of Christian charity.

My husband once went into court about lowering his child support payments when he got hurt at work, since he also had 2 other children to care for, and the judge actually told him that he should have gotten a lawyer to fight for him. But if he did, the judge would have figured that if he could afford a lawyer, he could afford to pay his child support. But because he didn't have a lawyer, his request for reduction was denied.

My husband got a job as a truck driver for one company that took out more than the legal amount of child support from his pay check (companies are only allowed to take a certain percentage of a pay check). When we went to court to show the Child Support agent that he actually received a negative pay check, the agent said "Oh, that's not legal. But we won't give you that money back."

A few years later, my husband got injured on the job and he couldn't work. So he called the Child Support Division to ask for a temporary reduction of his child support until he could go back to work. He paid the fee to go to court... and the judge put him in jail, stating he owed $1200 in back support, even though he had been paying on time for the past 3 years. It took me 12 days to get him out. My family would not help me, even though they could afford to; they believed he deserved to go to jail. Never mind that he had 2 other children – our children – to take care of, and he could not do that while he was incarcerated.

14
JOBS

John Ruskin once wrote 'The best grace is the consciousness that we have earned our dinner'.
LINUS

Though I have had my own business now for more than 17 years, I have had my share of interesting – and not so interesting – jobs besides. My very first job, believe it or not, was as a bus sitter. I bet there are very few people who can say that. One winter when I was about 14 years old, our school system tried an experiment; because of the lack of daylight hours during the winter, and the fact that the school boiler systems didn't work too reliably, someone came up with the brilliant idea of having the high school students go in earlier in the morning, and the elementary school kids after lunch (since both schools had to share the buses). The goal was to get the all of the students to and from school during daylight hours. But of course, since it got dark by 4:30 in January and February, they still needed to make sure the kids got home safely during that time. The "bus sitters" were junior high kids such as myself who sat on the buses for the elementary school students to make sure they got to their houses safely in the growing darkness.

After that, I worked where most kids my age did in the 80's… namely, I worked in fast food. And as it turns out, I was pretty good at it, since it required quite a lot of multi-tasking. It was also fun working with others my own age; at least for the first few years.

Until I went to work in fast food, I had thought of myself as an introvert; I could happily spend my days alone in my room, listening to music, reading or just plain day dreaming. And of course, I had my regular TV shows to watch each night, starting with *The Monkees* at 5 o'clock every weekday. Then, promptly at 8pm it was shows such as *Happy Days, Three's*

Company, Laverne and Shirley, and *Love Boat*, etc. I even had a brief obsession with *Battlestar Galactica.*

I picked up my work as a cashier quite quickly and easily, even occasionally receiving a tip from a guy if he'd come up to the counter more than once. I'd say something like "If I have to serve you again, you should at least give me a tip." And I'd usually get one. It turned out I was more of an extrovert than I thought.

I didn't start dating until then either, as it's rather difficult to find someone you're attracted to in a town that's full of guys you've known since the second grade… and my first "real" job was 3 towns over.

Throughout college, I held various work study jobs, including a semester each as a post office worker, a housekeeper (I cleaned toilets), a dish washer in the cafeteria… even waitressing for a few weeks in the Teacher's Lounge (a restaurant where only the professors ate). Each of these jobs were just a means to an end… basically, a way to pay for my laundry and a weekly pass for the subway, and not much else.

Once I graduated from college, I moved up to secretarial work. That was when I started to become more than a little restless. I had gone to college to become a Cinematographer, but I got married a few months after graduation instead. I tried my hand at being a Collection Secretary and a Filing Clerk at a law office. Needless to say, neither of those jobs lasted very long.

When my first husband and I moved to Florida, I even tried my hand working for Disney World – MGM Studios, to be precise. There, I was a glorified cashier (which meant I had to wear a costume) at one of their stores on the main thoroughfare. The most exciting thing about that job was being able to see a different movie star drive by during their daily parade (though none of them were A-list celebrities).

Until I worked for Disney, I had never been fired from, or quit a job, since every job I had ended because I had moved to another state (or it was a summer job during the college years). But after spending the summer wearing 2-inch heels on concrete floors, in a store that had yet to have its air conditioners installed, I got fed up enough that I just walked off one day and never came back. Let's just say that the working conditions there were not what you'd think they would be for the "happiest place on earth."

The most fun I had was as a desk clerk at a local motel along the main strip on the way to Disney World. I had no experience when they hired me, but again I caught on quickly. It was interesting getting to meet people from so many places around the world.

Eventually, I became the Night Auditor at that motel, but that wasn't as much fun as I had thought it would be, since I might check in 1 or 2 people during an 8-hour shift. I'd get my work done by 3 AM and have way too much time to stare at the clock, waiting until I could punch out. Once my biological clock told me that staying up all night wasn't a good idea, I left that job as well… to move back home to try and join the Army.

I had a bunch of other jobs during the time when I was homeless. Since I didn't have much of a wardrobe with me, I couldn't get work in any type of office setting, and at the time fast food places were mainly hiring teenagers, so my second husband (though we weren't married then), and I had to settle for temp jobs. Every afternoon we'd go to the temp agency and sit… and wait… hoping that the guy answering the phones would get a call for a job that we were qualified for… and that someone else wouldn't beat us to. Now I know how those illegal immigrants felt when they had to stand outside waiting for trucks to come by to ask for men to work the fields… desperately hoping that they'd be the ones to get on the truck before someone else did so that they could eat that day.

The first temp job we got ended up being the one we had for the longest period of time. It was at a plastic factory… something I didn't even realize existed until then. The first night we spent 8 hours stacking 2-liter empty Pepsi bottles onto pallets to be sent out to the Pepsi factory where they'd be filled with soda. Other nights I would inspect bleach bottles on one end of a huge green machine, while my man would place them in boxes and stack them on more pallets. I even spent one evening inspecting Kraft bottles as they went by on a conveyor belt; don't tell anyone, but I actually fell asleep standing up during that job once. That's when I knew that being pregnant didn't lend itself well to the night shift. Neither did the smell of the plastic. Eventually I had to stop going to that job for fear of hurting myself or my baby.

I tried my hand at a few other temp jobs after that: I remember 2 specifically. At one I had to put 5 different types of screws into a baggy while they went by me on a conveyor belt. That was incredibly mind-numbing! The other was working in a balloon factory, testing the balloons to make sure they didn't have holes in them. Basically, I had hope that none of the balloons were defective; otherwise, they would pop in my face. Do I have to say that I never went back to *that* job?

I wish I could say that during that time, I bore homelessness with strength and dignity. I most definitely did not. And though I was pregnant, I cannot blame all of my behavior on hormones. I had never felt so scared and alone in my life! Even once we finally made enough money for us to stay in a hotel most nights, I was usually depressed and complaining about something. I wished only to go back home to the safety of my family, where everything would be alright again.

I will never look at a homeless person the same again.

And it was then that I realized that security really is just an illusion.

After my mother passed away, I decided our family needed a change. We found a woman online – one of the authors I worked with – who said she was putting her house up for sale on a rent-to-own basis. It sounded like an awesome opportunity for us. So we took a long weekend and checked out the house. It was a shot-gun house, built in the 1800's. It was beautiful and full of charm and possibilities... and it was in our price range. So a few months later, we moved in.

Only our new landlord had moved out two weeks before, and she left her 4 dogs and cat named Stinky in the house for us to care for. Two years later, a gentleman drove up to the house and asked us what we were doing there. When we told him we were renting from the owner, he said "But I am the owner. My ex-wife did not win the house in the divorce." We were lucky he gave us some time to find another place to live.

A few months after we moved in, the "landlord" had her girlfriend come and take the 4 dogs to her house. The next morning, our youngest son woke up covered in welts; it looked like he had a form of chicken pox, from his head to his toes. It turns out, when the dogs were removed from the house, their fleas stayed... and they settled on my son, whose bed was the lowest to the ground. We had to shave his head and give him Benadryl and antibiotics to keep him from getting an infection, since there were so many bites. We did bomb the house – twice – but the fleas just would not die.

THE DOCTOR IS IN
Advice from Lucy Van Pelt

CHARLIE BROWN: Do you think I can ever become
a mature and well-adjusted person?
LUCY: For a question like that, I have to be paid in advance.
CHARLIE BROWN: In advance?! Why?
LUCY: Because I don't think you're going to like the answer.

When I was a kid, my mother once accused me of having a "Peter Pan Complex." When I asked her what that meant, she said that I did not want to grow up. And she was right. I saw no benefit in being an adult. Grown-ups had to go to work 5 out of 7 days a week, get up early, pay bills, and they still had others above them to cater to. Not to mention being responsible for the lives and well-being of their children. Nope, I was determined that that was not going to be me!

I took this a step further by refusing to wear the first bra my mother gave me. No matter that the rest of my girlfriends were already wearing one.

The only good things I could see about being an adult were (1) no one could tell you when to go bed – I could stay up all night if I wanted to (forget how I'd feel in the morning, of course), and (2) I could eat what I wanted to (unless I had children who would catch me doing it). And of course, I didn't have to go to school. Then again, at least when you were in school, you were there with others your age, all who also had to be there… so there was some comfort in being trapped there all together for a few hours a day. But at least with school, you got weekends and holidays off.. and of course, 3 months during the summer!

What did being mature and well-adjusted get a person anyway? A house with a husband (or wife) and 2.5 kids with a white picket fence on a suburban street and a retirement watch at 70? Nope, that life was definitely not meant for me.

CHARLIE BROWN: What can you do when you don't fit in? What can you do when life seems to be passing you by?
LUCY: Follow me… I want to show you something. (Stops on a hill) See the horizon over there? See how big this world is? See how much room there is for everybody? Have you ever seen any other worlds?
CHARLIE BROWN: No.
LUCY: As far as you know this is the only world there is… right?
CHARLIE BROWN: Right.
LUCY: There are no other worlds for you to live in… right?
CHARLIE BROWN: Right.
LUCY: You were born to live in this world… right?
CHARLIE BROWN: Right.
LUCY: Well, LIVE IN IT, THEN!! (Charlie Brown falls over backwards) Five cents, please…

This goes to show one of the most fundamental aspects of Charlie Brown… he does not feel as if he fits in. How many of us have felt that way at one time or another? For me, I felt like this for most of my life. But in Lucy's not-so-subtle way, she sets Charlie Brown straight by letting him know he DOES fit in…that each and every one of us is here for a reason – a purpose – and to stop griping about it and start living, already! Ironically, when everyone is telling you "don't sweat the small stuff," it's those very "small" moments that can make the difference in someone's life, including your own.

CHARLIE BROWN: I have deep feelings of depression.
LUCY: Snap out of it! Five cents, please.

After my first son was born, I was diagnosed with clinical depression. Apparently, that meant that I was going to be permanently depressed, but that my hormones were out of whack from the pregnancy (others would call it post-partum depression), and that a little therapy and some medication would do the trick. So I started taking anti-depressants.

A few years later, after the birth of my second son, I had to go back into therapy for the same reason. Though this therapist said that there was something in my brain chemistry that lends itself to depression… that apparently I had a history of it. That certainly wasn't good news. But I knew that I was hurting my family by having such severe mood swings, so once again I agreed to take the prescribed medication.

Today I have come to realize that most people have a sort of clinical depression, as that comes from the fact that our lives are so disconnected. We spend way too much time in front of the television or bent over cell phones, texting and talking to everyone but those who are right in front of us. When did this happen? I was not brought up this way! And yet we tend to go out to eat more than we stay in, since that is the only way the entire family will sit down together at a table and talk to each other. The kitchen table used to be the center of the family; today it is mostly used as a catch-all for papers and things we drop there as we walk through the door.

Ever since I started meditating – and I admit I cannot do it for more than a minute at a time, even after years of practice – I no longer have severe mood swings. Sure, I will feel sad now and then, but it is normal sadness. And I've learned to embrace those feelings, instead of trying to hide them or feel guilty for them, and they pass much more quickly than they used to. And I am no longer a drama queen… meaning I no longer feel this deep-seated need to start up drama for the sake of it, no matter who it may hurt. It actually bothers me if I don't settle problems I have with someone quickly, rather than holding it in and letting my feelings of hurt or anger fester.

It always bothered me that we seem to grow up being taught that our human emotions are things to be hidden or tamed, as if we were not given the whole range of emotions for good reason.. and that reason was to USE them… to learn, to grow, and to LIVE!

PART II

THE CAST

SNOOPY

My husband often reminds me of Charlie Brown's Snoopy. Though Snoopy is, of course, a dog, he tends to think of himself as human, often getting into trouble much like a typical guy would do. In general, Snoopy is a loveable character, very loyal to his friends. But he is also easily hurt. And let's face it, he's a little bossy. But you can't help but love his indomitable spirit, his loyalty and his inability to worry about what others think of him. If he wants to accomplish something, he simply sets out to get it done, sometimes in very imaginative or unexpected ways.

Snoopy is also often the comic relief in Charlie Brown's world. Plus, he tends to draw others to him, not the least of which is Woodstock, his faithful bird companion.

Of course, we also can't forget that Snoopy is a bit of a daredevil (the World War I flying ace comes to mind). And when he is in a social setting, he's usually the life of the party.

But no matter what the situation, Snoopy is not only in the thick of it; he is usually the instigator.

When I met my husband, the first words I said to him were "You are so obnoxious." At the time, he was reveling an audience of co-workers about his various adventures during a break at a temporary night job. When I said those words to him, my husband put his hands behind his head, and his feet up on the table in the break room. He smiled and said, "I know." Thus began our unusual courtship.

When we met, we were both actually married to other people. I am not proud to say it, but our friendship turned into much more than that a lot more quickly than I could have anticipated.

Like Snoopy, my husband is constantly keeping me on my toes. I still don't always know quite what to expect from him. He can spend days puttering around the house, doing not much of anything, and then suddenly come up with an idea of how to make something out of bits and scraps he's got around the house, or he has an idea for us to go on an adventure. And once he gets something in his head, there's nothing that will stop him from accomplishing it. He's used to working alone, but he has no problem fitting into nearly any crowd of people, no matter their faith, financial or political status. And if he's into a project, he can easily forget that everyone around him exists.

He has often had to pull me out of my own shell, as I tend to be more of a loner. But even though he enjoys laughing at me now and then, his laughter is never meant to be mean. Much like Snoopy, he is sometimes honest to a fault. But no matter what, I could not imagine Charlie Brown without Snoopy… the same as I cannot imagine life without my husband.

LINUS

"Learning to ignore things is one of the great
paths to inner peace."
LINUS

My oldest son tends to remind me of Linus, Charlie Brown's best friend. Though he is younger than Charlie Brown, in many ways he seems older, as he is usually the voice of wisdom – sometimes even the philosopher – of the group. He also has a belief system that is different from everyone else's: who doesn't remember Linus' long waits in the pumpkin patch on Halloween, waiting for the Great Pumpkin while everyone else was out trick-or-treating? He tolerates his older sister, Lucy, mostly out of fear. And he tries to avoid Sally, Charlie Brown's sister, since he knows she likes him… and he is just not interested, and he's not the type of kid to say or do something mean just to get her off his back.

In many ways, the relationship I have with my oldest son is much like that of Linus and Charlie Brown. When he was little, my son's father was often on the road, leaving us, along with his little brother, home alone. So we spent a lot of time together. And eventually, as he got older, he became my confidante, since there were many days that I didn't have anyone else to talk to. We have a lot in common, including our love for the written word… and our addiction to video games. We can spend hours watching TV shows or waxing philosophical about life, writing, his art, and spirituality.

My oldest son also has an older half-sister who he begrudgingly admires – and who he is more than little afraid of. And he was always keenly disinterested in girls who were younger than him, often referring to them simply as "immature and silly." But he is loyal to a fault, and he does not let the opinion of others dissuade him in his beliefs.

My son is also not one to aim for material things. Much like Linus, he believes that the most important things in life are free: knowledge, friendship and family.

Ironically, Linus' signature prop, his ever-present blanket, was something that I myself had when I was little. I took that blanket everywhere with me… until my mother slowly cut it down into smaller and smaller pieces… and eventually "lost" the rest in order to rid me of it. So I can definitely relate to Linus.

LUCY

LUCY: *I'm intrigued by this view you
have on the purpose of life,*
CHARLIE BROWN. *You say we're put on this
earth to make others happy? ...
What are the others put here for?*

I am the oldest of 7 children: 2 biological and 5 of them adopted. My biological sister often reminds me of Lucy. It's never really said whether or not Lucy is older than Charlie Brown – I believe they are supposed to be the same age – but she often acts as if she is older. Lucy is intelligent, self-confidant, and she has no problem letting others know her opinion on a variety of topics. Yet she seems to always be on a quest to find out what makes others tick – hence, her 5 cent psychiatrist booth. She says what she thinks and doesn't apologize for it. Though most of us loved to hate Lucy, I believe that we can also relate to her and many of her thoughts on how the world should work. And ultimately she does seem to have a good heart… as well as a good sense of humor.

When I was growing up, I looked up to my sister – though I never told her that. She was beautiful and confidant, and I often felt intimidated around her, even though I was a few years older than her. We didn't have a lot in common, other than our enjoyment of Barbie dolls and the love for our pets.

As we got older and we both moved away from home, we would have long phone conversations on a variety of subjects, and most of the time I'd end up laughing with her at the way she'd describe something that ticked her off. I was not always sure that I could bring up certain topics with her, as she had very strong opinions about many of them, and she did not hesitate to let me know them. Yet, she always seemed to be willing to listen to my side of things, even if she disagreed with me.

When my mother contracted cancer and she began to make preparations for her own passing, instead of going to me, she relied on my sister to become her Executor, as she is much more of a "take charge" kind of person – more organized and less emotional – than I am. It seemed to be the logical choice.

As it is in many families, ours is a love-hate relationship. But I still respect her and admire the woman she has become today.

SALLY

SALLY: *Sorry to wake you up, Big Brother,*
but I've been thinking. I have begun to doubt the
existence of the tooth fairy. Is it wrong to lie awake at
night thinking about such things?
CHARLIE BROWN: *Only if you expect an answer.*
SALLY: *I'll go ask your dog.*

Sally is Charlie Brown's little sister, though in many ways she seems older than him, often coming out with her own little bursts of wisdom that make us think. She is a no-nonsense girl, who is always in search of answers to the bigger questions. She has her own way of presenting herself, and is not afraid to go against the status quo, often irritating her teachers with her questions – usually during her Show and Tell presentations. She can definitely hold her own. And though she does often pick on her older brother, she is also fiercely loyal of him when push comes to shove.

I have often thought of one of my adopted sisters as Sally. Though we didn't live together for long, since I graduated college before she was even in high school, she has always been an important part of my life. And though she has said that she admires me in many ways, she is also quick to point out when I am full of crap… and for that I am grateful to her. With her, I always know exactly where I stand.

That said, she doesn't take anything at face value. She takes the time to learn all she can about a person or topic before stating an opinion, and she respects the fact that others may not agree with her. And if they don't, she really doesn't care; a character trait I sorely wish to emulate.

The above quote also reflects a large part of my sister's personality, as she was the one who had always questioned the existence of God, or other things unseen, even from a very young age, or so she's told me (sitting in church, knowing that much of what she heard just didn't make a lot of sense). She is the first one in our family to see the inconsistencies...and downright hypocrisy...of religion... another big reason why I admire her.

SCHROEDER

LUCY: *So you forgot Beethoven's birthday?*
What difference does it make?
Who really cares? It's all so stupid!
You take these things too seriously.
Now if it had been MY birthday you had forgotten...
SCHROEDER: *Oh, good grief!*

My biological brother has many of the attributes of Schroeder, the ever-playing pianist of the Charlie Brown gang. Schroeder doesn't say much in words; he tends to let his music do the talking for him. And he doesn't seem to like confrontation, though he can make it obvious in his own way when he's upset about something. It seems he is happiest when he is doing his own thing; mainly, playing his music. But he does also have a sociable side.

Since Lucy and Schroeder are often seen together, this reminds me of the fact that my sister and brother have always been closer than I've been with either of them. I attribute a lot of that to the fact that I am 4 years older than my sister, and 8 years older than my brother – so they did spend more of their childhood years together than I got to with either of them – but a part of me has always rather envied the fact that they were so close. Now that they are older, though, they seem to have more of the love-hate relationship that Lucy and Schroeder have.

The biggest similarity between my brother and Schroeder is that he has always been the artist of the group. From a very young age, my brother could paint and draw beautiful scenes that were the envy of all of us… though of course we are also very proud of him. Yet he usually chose not to sell those paintings, because they became such a part of him… much like Schroeder and his music.

My brother has never been one to enjoy confrontation, preferring to let others sort out their differences themselves. He would also prefer to be left alone somewhere with his art, though admittedly I have never seen him play a piano. But similar to Schroeder, he is never one to be left out of a party, and he does seem to get along well enough with everyone, human and dog alike.

WOODSTOCK

WOODSTOCK: *[squawk noises]*
SNOOPY: *No, that's not a star... it's a comet.*
WOODSTOCK: *[squawk noises]*
SNOOPY: *How do I know? It says so on the side...*
WOODSTOCK: *[squawk noises]*
SNOOPY: *He never believes anything I tell him.*

Since Woodstock doesn't speak a language we are familiar with, his words have been reduced above to squawk noises. Woodstock is Snoopy's best friend. They two of them are often seen together, cooking up various schemes in their search for fun... or payback, as the case may be. Sometimes it's even Woodstock who comes up with the ideas, and Snoopy happily plays along. And though Woodstock cannot speak, it's usually pretty obvious what he's trying to say. And he is no pushover, either... he will call Snoopy out if the dog forgets he's there or does something he thinks isn't right.

My younger son has never been able speak, but he has no problem getting his point across in most instances. Like Woodstock, he is usually laid back and happy – he can often be seen dancing in his room to the music on one of his DVDs – but he can occasionally be in a bad mood... and when he is, the feathers will fly! And similarly, like the infamous picture of Woodstock hanging out with Snoopy on the top of his dog house, my son can usually be found with his father (also known as Snoopy), the two of them happily goofing off, relaxing or cooking up some scheme together. They are definitely brothers-in-arms.

PEPPERMINT PATTY

*"That was a hard test, Marcie. I didn't know if it was
an essay test, True or False, or multiple choice.
I just put down 'Not Guilty'."*
PEPPERMINT PATTY

Peppermint Patty was the tom-boy of the group. She was a no-nonsense, down-to-earth girl who did not wear makeup or wear dresses. And she was usually seen with her friend Marci trailing closely behind her. Both of them, as you know, had a crush on Charlie Brown.

I actually had a girlfriend in high school that was eerily like Peppermint Patty. She was definitely the tom-boy of our group. She played softball on her local team. Though she was interested in sports, her main passion was horses. That was mainly what she talked about. And when she had an idea about something, she would hang on to it for dear life.

Interestingly enough, in our junior year of high school, my friend found her own Marci, when a new girl came to town. Those two were rarely seen apart, at least when they were in school together. Believe it or not, they usually sat in the classroom the same way that Peppermint Patty and Marci were always depicted – with Peppermint Patty in front of Marci. And they did always seem to have an interest in the same guys.

MARCI

PEPPERMINT PATTY: *So what are you doing, Marci?*
MARCI: *Just lying in bed reading.*
PEPPERMINT PATTY: *Do you wear your glasses
when you're sleeping?*
MARCI: *Sure, so I can see what I'm dreaming.*
PEPPERMINT PATTY: *There's no doubt in my mind,
Marci, that you are excessively weird.*

Marci was Peppermint Patty's best friend. The two of them seemed to be inseparable, even sharing their like of the same boy – Charlie Brown (Marci called him "Charles") – though Marci kind of kept that information from Peppermint Patty, for the most part.

Doesn't there always seems to be that one person in a group who tags along wherever you go, regardless of whether they were invited or not? That's what Marci makes me think of. In high school, that friend was the new girl who joined our group in junior high. She, too, had a very different way of looking at the world. She also gave me and my four other close friends, original nicknames.

On our street, that girl was my next door neighbor. Her mother and my mother were long-time friends, so we were often shoved together while they visited, even if it was not something that either of us wanted, since we were the same age. I remember many an afternoon when I had to try to find something for her and I to do that that might interest her. Though over time, I kind of came to enjoy our get-togethers, because she had a unique way of looking at the world. Many a time we would end up laughing over the silliest things, not the least of which was the antics of our younger brothers and sisters.

PIG PEN

FRIEDA: *You're an absolute mess. Just look at yourself.*
PIG PEN: [L*ooks at himself in Frieda's mirror and smiles*]
On the contrary, I didn't think I looked THAT good.

Pig Pen is known for his perpetually dirty overalls and the cloud of dust that seems to surround him at all times. He isn't a major character in the Charlie Brown gang, but he is an important mainstay.

One of my youngest adopted brothers fits the bill of this character. It's not so much that he's actually, physically dirty like Pig Pen (though he has been seen that way on occasion), but he travels down a road of life that is a lot "dirtier" than the rest of us would take. He has had his problems with addictions, as well as much loss in his earlier life, yet I can't remember many days when I didn't see a smile on his face. He seems to take all that life throws at him, no matter how "dirty" and throw it right back in life's face, happily dancing through it all whenever he has a chance. Like Pig Pen, he seems to have a very big opinion of himself, no matter what anyone else might say otherwise. And similar to the Charlie Brown gang, who had to put a certain amount of distance between themselves and Pig Pen, the same can be said for my brother, who often keeps people at arm's length in his own life.

THE ADULTS

ADULT: *Wah, wah, wah.*
CHARLIE BROWN: *Yes, ma'am.*

In the animated series of Charlie Brown, none of the adults are heard or seen by the audience, other than the occasional shot of one of their legs. When a parent or teacher does speak, we don't even hear the actual words they say; we are left to decipher the rather unique "wha-wha-wha" they make when they speak by the replies made by the characters. I'm not sure why this was the case, but at least we know that the Charlie Brown gang did have parents and other adults who were responsible for them.

Obviously, when I was growing up, my own parents were a very large part of my life, though my mother has been gone now for over a decade.

I did not get along very well with my father. I think that being a female, I was rather a mystery to him. He simply had no idea how to contend with me. So he left most of the child-rearing to my mother. Though I never felt as if he neglected me; he was just more of a silent, solid presence for me.

For most of my life, my mother and I were close. I was her first born, after all. My sister was born 4 years after me, and my brother 4 years after that, so she was able to give me a lot of attention.

As I got older, I shared things with my mother that most kids didn't. I told her all my hopes and dreams, about the boys I had crushes on… even the first time I French-kissed a boy.

My mother was what I would call "Super Mom". Sure, she cooked and cleaned, but how many moms could also make clothes, decorate cakes, design and create Cabbage Patch kids and Raggedy Ann and Andy dolls (which she sold for extra cash), plant gardens, draw up plans for renovations to the house (including a fireplace and a large deck in the backyard), and take time out to play with us in the pool during the summer? I don't think I ever saw her relax for more than 10 minutes at a time. She was always doing something – knitting, crocheting, folding laundry, baking cookies, cakes or pies, rearranging the furniture or making plans to expand the house. Even when she was taking care of 2 to 5 foster children who were 4 years of age and under, she was also taking care of the house, paying the bills, entertaining company, scheduling doctor's appointments, or helping us with homework.

Christmas in our home was always full of laughter, good food, lots of family, and tons of presents. Summers were long, sunny days of splashing in the pool, Kool-Aid and homemade ice pops and hot dogs and hamburgers on the grill. We were the house that all the kids hung out at. It was rare to have an entire day when someone didn't come over.

I can't tell you how many times I heard people say "Your mother is a saint." I would shake my head and reply "No… she's just crazy." And I meant that in the best possible way. My mother has left me was wonderful, lasting memories that I will cherish forever.

PART III

"Good grief!"

1
HIT AND RUN

In a classic example of how my life had been up to this point, just as things started to look up, that proverbial ball once again got pulled out from under my feet. I could not count how many times in my life that I was hit with something when I was already down. Charlie Brown's popular response of "Good grief" would sum it up nicely.

After we were basically fired from our Family Teacher position, my younger brother offered to take us in to his home in Florida. It was a miracle that he even had the space for 2 adults and 2 children. So, broken and defeated, we used the last of our money to purchase a van and throw what we owned into it to drive to his home. We even had to spend Thanksgiving day on the road.

Once again, we had to figure out how to make a living. I still had my home business, but it was definitely not going to get us through. So I went to work part-time at a family restaurant while my husband began the search for work.

A few months after we moved in, my sister-in-law got another job opportunity and they decided to move to the very state we had just moved away from. Thankfully, they let us stay in the house as caretakers while we got back on our feet. Though my brother wasn't asking us for rent, it was still a struggle for us to get by.

Then my husband got a job! It was his first in over 2 years, since his surgery (we couldn't count the Family Teaching job, as we hadn't had a chance to actually care for any foster kids before we were kicked off the reservation, as it were). And it paid enough that I could quit my part-time job and stay home with the kids.

A few weeks in, it was the end of the month and my husband got paid. Once I finished paying the bills, I realized that we actually had money left over! I was so excited that I went straight to our bank and opened up a savings account… the first one we'd had in over 8 years.

The very next morning – and this is no joke – I received a phone call. It was the hospital in Orlando telling me that my husband had been in an accident and that he was about to go into surgery. He had been hit by a truck – it was a hit and run – thrown 10 yards into the grass on the side of the highway, and left for dead. Ironically, it was a truck driver who found him and called 911. He had broken his pelvis, both legs and he had a huge gouge in his right side from the vehicle that hit him. They wanted to take his legs, but my husband made sure to let me know that that wasn't an option.

So that money that I had just put into the savings account… it had to be taken right back out of the bank to pay the tow service for us to get our truck back.

If that wasn't enough, we had no insurance, since he hadn't yet worked for 30 full days. And since he had just got off of work – he had stopped by the side of the road to walk around so that he didn't fall asleep at the wheel – there would be no workman's comp. We were alone in Florida, with no family nearby – no support system – living on borrowed time in my brother's house with only the income from my small business to keep us afloat.

Needless to say, this was one of the lowest times in our lives. I was in constant fear that the phone would ring and it would be the hospital telling me that my husband didn't make it through his latest surgery (he would have more than 60 operations in the next 2 months). And I had to keep a brave face on for my boys.

I had never prayed so much in my life. Yet I had also never felt so alone. It felt as if God was just not listening.

One night I could not sleep. My husband had called a few hours earlier, crying because he was in so much pain. I felt so helpless, so utterly hopeless… there was no way I was going to get any sleep after that.

I had rented an obscure movie from the video store that day, so I decided to watch it. I had seen a preview of it a few nights before on another video I had rented. It was called "Conversations with God." The title intrigued me.

I put it in. Halfway through the movie, there was a scene where the main character, Neale, was in a very low point in his own life (this was based on a true story), and he had been praying incessantly, the same as I had. And then, at 4:31 AM, God spoke to Neale, saying, "Do you really want answers to the questions you are asking, or are you just venting?"

During the rest of the scene, God began to speak to Neale about many of the issues that he had been worrying about… issues regarding suffering, success, money, love and so much more.

As I watched, I began to cry in great, gulping sobs. For the first time in my life, I felt as if God was speaking directly to me… that this movie had been put in front of me at the exact right time for me to hear this message. And that message that God was trying to give me was: "YOU GOT ME ALL WRONG." God was *not* made in the image of humans, which is really what the God of Christianity was – just a larger, more powerful version of us, with all the same personality traits, including anger and jealousy – but WE were made in the image of GOD… meaning we were *part* of God… or Gods ourselves, in a manner of speaking. What a revelation!

From that moment on, my life began to change. It was as if a huge weight had been lifted from my heart. I had never felt such incredible PEACE. Time no longer seemed to matter. I would find myself looking out a window at nature and reveling in the smallest of things… an ant crawling up a tree; the sound of birds singing in the trees; the play of dust in the sun's rays. Everything seemed so new and miraculous!

Gone was all the fear over my husband's condition, or the worry about where we'd get the money to eat, pay our bills, or buy the gas needed to visit him in the hospital (which was 40 miles away). Somehow, deep down, I knew that we would make it through this. I was beginning to realize that fear and worry were wasted emotions.

The next morning, I remember going into the store at one of the gas stations near the house. When I walked into the building, instead of putting my head down and worrying about what people were thinking of me – as I had unconsciously done my entire life – I held my head up high. I looked people in the eye and smiled… genuinely smiled at them. And the response I got was amazing! They would look right back at me, and smile as well. It was as if they could sense that there was something different about me.

Time seemed to speed up and slow down randomly. I found I could go outside and sit amidst nature for hours, simply reveling in the beauty of creation; enjoying the feel of the sun on my face and the sound of the wind rustling through the trees. And my problems no longer seemed insurmountable. I was learning to live in the moment.

I began to read books on spirituality voraciously; anything I could get my hands on. Of course, the first books I read were the *Conversations with God* series by Neale Donald Walsh. But others who inspired me were Deepak Chopra, Debbie Ford… even Oprah Winfrey. And their messages were all basically the same… WE ARE ALL ONE (we are all made up of the same "stuff"), and LOVE IS ALL THERE IS.

And the most amazing thing about all of this was that, as I explored all these new ideas about God… that made perfect sense to me, no less… the words that Jesus spoke suddenly took on a whole new, miraculous meaning. For the first time in my life I realized what an incredible man Jesus was… ironic as I know that sounds. Once I concentrated solely on Jesus' message, things began to make much more sense. For Jesus had been trying to tell people how they could realize their own divinity… that we are all members of the body of God [John 17:22]. But if they couldn't believe that, for that seemed so far-fetched, they could instead consider themselves a part of *him*, as *he* was part of God… and by default, that meant we ALL were part of God [John 17:23, 26]. It was such a marvelous message, yet that seemed to get warped somehow by every minister I have ever heard speak over the years.

It is so ironic that the moment I decided not to follow Christianity… or any religion, for that matter… that Jesus' words had so much more meaning in my life.

Still, I knew instinctively that I shouldn't be "following" Jesus, or spending my time worshiping God… but that my spiritual journey was to start… and always come from… *within myself.* That God was not some super-human sitting up in the sky on his throne, passing judgement on us. God was SO much bigger than that!

I was suddenly free to love myself without condition, faults and all. And because of this, I no longer felt the need to blame anyone else for my problems. For the first time, I took ownership of everything that had happened to me in my life up to this point. Even the horrible accident my husband had… I knew it was something we had both agreed to experience together before we came into this life…perhaps not him specifically getting hit by a truck, but we were supposed to have this kind of challenge in our marriage.

My marriage also improved, at least from my perspective, as I no longer put the burden of my happiness onto my husband. I realized that it had never been his responsibility to make me happy in the first place. My happiness had to come from *within.*

And so it did. As I continued to learn and grow spiritually, meditating for the first time in my life, an indescribable joy would suddenly bubble up from within me for no apparent reason at the most unexpected times. Though outwardly it didn't seem as if my life as improving, that wasn't as important as what I was experiencing within myself. Sometimes a feeling of pure bliss would overcome me as I was driving down the road, and I would find myself laughing with joy, knowing deep in my soul that all was exactly as it was meant to be at that moment.

Another significant change occurred after I had this epiphany about God. I stopped praying to God… or at least I stopped asking God for things. That insinuated that we were having a one-sided conversation. Instead, I *communed* with God, practicing the art of silence, so I could listen to God's speaking back to me. It wasn't exactly meditation, for I was not very good at that, but I learned later on that it was a kind of "active" meditation… as long as I stayed in the moment as much as possible, positive things would start to happen more and more frequently. Every question I ever wanted answered I had no doubt would be answered… if I took the time to listen. No more of this "Oh, God must have said no – that was his will" kind of thing when I didn't get something I had asked for. The whole point was not to ask at all, but to THANK God for all that I currently had. And not to worry about what I didn't have. To live in the moment as much as possible.

Sometimes the answers from God would come to me as that still, small voice inside that we all have. Many people refer to that as our intuition, but it's the same as God speaking to us, since we are just bits of God having a human experience. But many times the message would come in the words of a song I was listening to on the radio, or in the words of advice from a friend, or from a scene in a movie. I was starting to see so much synchronicity in my life that it was incredible.

If we blew a tire, my first thought wouldn't be "Why me?" or some other negative response. Instead, it was be something like "It'll be fine." Or "Okay, another adventure." And sure enough, we'd drive by an auto store that was having a sale on our size tires… with no waiting! Or we'd be low on funds for an event for my son's school, and my husband would find money on the ground on the way into the store…. Just enough for us to buy what we needed.

While we were living at that house, the heating system died and the "landlord" refused to fix it. So we had to use the old wood stove in the kitchen to heat the entire house. We would spend hours a day chopping, stacking and feeding wood into the stove to keep warm. One day we spent a few hours collecting these huge cedar beams that were in the old barn. We put the saw in the doorway of the barn and cut until we could no longer feel our fingers. A few hours later, as we were about to go to bed, we heard this huge "WHOOSH" noise that we could not identify. In the morning, we woke up to see that the entire barn had collapsed in upon itself from the weight of the snow that had fallen that day. How lucky we were that we were not in the barn when that happened!

During that winter, we got a barrel to burn odds and ends in when we worked outside. My husband set it up near the circular driveway and put a few holes in it for circulation. Then he put one cup on gasoline at the bottom, along with some wood. We had a nice fire. A few hours later, he took the hose and doused the fire, then put a cover on the barrel. A few days later, he took the cover off and dropped a few small branches into the barrel... they immediately caught on fire, without us using a match. Again, we doused the barrel with water until the flames were out, then covered it. Every single time we uncovered the barrel, all we needed to do was add one piece of wood and the fire would start again, without us adding any matches or gasoline to the barrel. Eventually, we began to call it "the barrel from hell."

2
TO BUY OR NOT TO BUY

If you live on this planet, unless you are living under a rock, or in a third-world country, there is no way to avoid being constantly bombarded by consumerism. It seems as if every single person you meet is trying to sell you something. Every television show you watch has more and more commercials then actual content; magazines are full of more ads than articles of substance; billboards for cosmetics, time shares, soft drinks, designer clothing, or the newest video game system, cell phone or laptop are everywhere. Life seems to be like a giant game to keep us occupied in acquiring more and more things in order to compete with the guy next door. And for what? No matter how much we acquire, it never seems to be enough. And it certainly doesn't seem to make people any happier.

This constant marketing also leaves most of us with this general feeling of lack. I know, because I have felt it for most of my life as well. I also had phases where I collected things: decorative plates; ceramic houses; anything having to do with wolves; M&M tins, native American paraphernalia. I still have a small collection of Coca-Cola collectibles, but I only want what I can use or display in my house.

These days I can honestly say that THINGS no longer have much of a hold on me. They are simply not a priority in my life. I can go to a retail store or a flea market and see all the things that I *used* to think I had to have… and bypass them quite easily. Even if I see a Coca-Cola item, I can enjoy the fact that I've seen it, but I can take it or leave it. For me, it's more enjoyable to go to a yard sale than to a mall, because I can scour the area for those unexpected treasures… the beautiful blue chair that I use for reading in my bedroom; the Coca-Cola tea light I use when the power is out; 2 picture frames to put my book covers in when I hang them on the wall. And if I buy something that I enjoyed for a brief time and no longer have the need for, I can just as easily give it away or sell

121

it at our own yard sale. It kind of saddens me when I see someone with a cart full of things that you know they won't use a few months from now, even if they even use it in the first place.

I like the idea of recycling as well. It's much more enjoyable for me to give money to a neighbor when I buy a few used shirts at his yard sale then it is to buy a $20 brand new shirt at the local Wal-Mart… even if there is a small stain under the armpit. Not only is that something that won't be thrown into the dump, but I'm helping someone else make some much needed extra money. Saving money while saving resources – you can't beat that.

I have never been one who had to have the "latest" anything, but there is just so much for sale out there that is just plain not needed. It's one thing to buy a video game for $30 that you will spend hours playing (until you get tired of it and trade it in toward the next game); it's another to have to have the latest video game system, when you already have 3 others; or you feel the need to buy a new car every few years, or trade up for the newest cell phone every 6 months; or own 30 pairs of shoes. I own 3 pairs of shoes at any given time, and I don't buy a new pair until mine wear out completely. I will even buy a $2 pair of sneakers at a yard sale to use for mowing – why spend more for a new pair that's just going to get dirty anyway? I am probably one of the few people under 70 these days who doesn't even own a cell phone. A landline is just fine for me, thanks.

I may be a dreamer, but I believe that we could live without more than half of the products that are made today. If all the clothing, car and electronics factories stopped producing today, the entire world would still have enough to cloth to clothe every single person, give every driver a car, every family a house, and every person who needed one a computer and/or cell phone for the next 5 years. Heaven forbid we should FIX things when they break instead of throwing them out and using that as an excuse to buy a new one. Am I right?

Once we moved to our new home, just 3 miles down the street from the previous one, we got a cat of our own. He loved to play in our back yard, since we had an acre of land. We also had quite a few small, cute bunnies that lived on the property. And a few rather large snakes. Eventually, my husband killed the 3 largest snakes. In the spring, we saw that the bunnies, free from the fear of any predators, had grown immensely. They were now bigger than our cat. So when we pointed out "Kris, bunnies!" the cat took one look at the huge rabbit and fled into the house.

We had bought a small frog for our younger son. We put it in a fish bowl. To keep it away from the cat, we had put a piece of plastic wrap over the top, with a few puncture holes for air, and a small plastic frog on top of that to keep the plastic on. One morning we got up and the frog was gone. We would have blamed it on the cat, except for the fact that the plastic wrap – and the small frog – was still on top of the fish bowl. We never did figure out what happened to that frog.

3
SPIRIT ANIMALS

*"Why can't I have a normal dog
like everyone else?"*
CHARLIE BROWN

Part of my continuing spiritual search led me back to my interest in Native American culture… or as many refer to it – The Red Road. So I began once again to study the Native American myths and legends. As you probably know, animals are a very large part of Native American culture. So I took a particular interest in how animals.. in particular, how important having animal spirit guides were to Native American culture.

I had always had an affinity for dolphins. When I was young, I would collect anything having to do with dolphins (t-shirts, knick-knacks, posters). According to Native American culture, the dolphin represents joyful play and love for family. This does seem to coincide with a spirit animal that I would have had in my youth. Plus, I have always loved the water. I was taught how to swim at the Boys and Girls Club in the city where I was born. And when my parents got a small 4-foot deep pool in our back yard, I was in heaven. I spent many summer days, hour after hour, in the pool; whether I was alone or with others didn't matter. Even today, swimming is still my favorite activity.

As I got older, my affinity for dolphins transferred to the wolves. In Native American culture, the wolf represents loyalty for family, as well as intelligence and trusting one's instincts. But it is also a powerful symbol of freedom. I have always put my family first, but I have also felt restless most of my life, never wanting to settle down in one place for too long. I can also relate to the symbol of the lone wolf, as I tend to prefer to be alone (if given the choice).

After my husband's accident, and I started along my spiritual path in earnest, the owl became an important part of my life. I never thought I would live somewhere where I could see owls every single day; in fact, I don't remember really seeing an owl up close in the wild until then. But once we moved from my brother's house to rent a mobile home, it turns out the land we were on was part of nature Preserve... and we had our own family of barred owls in our own front yard!

At first, I was intimidated by the owls that made a home in one of the owl houses the landlord had set up 30+ feet high in one of our willow trees. But when the owls that were nesting there had a baby, I soon became obsessed with watching them. I named the baby Wheezy, after the sound that she made when she was nervous. And eventually she became so comfortable with me that she'd play a kind of hide and seek with me, watching and waiting until I found her in the tree she was sitting on before she'd move on to another.

Owls are very private by nature. They like to house their nests in an area that is undisturbed by humans... and they don't allow other predatory animals or birds to live in the area when they are nesting. They promptly kicked out the woodpeckers who were living in our willow trees once their baby was born.

So it came as no surprise to me when I found out that the owl represents a deep connection with wisdom and intuitive knowledge. It seemed as if my interest in various animals throughout my life was mirroring my inner spiritual journey! The very fact that such solitary, independent birds would allow me to sit near them while they hunted... and not attack me when I got too close to their baby as she was learning how to fly... told me that these owls could sense this connection, and they knew instinctively that I would not harm them. The father owl even sat in our driveway one day as we all got into the van... he didn't fly away as we drove right past him... he simply swiveled his head 360 degrees and watched us go.

As I continued to study spirit animals, I found out that in Shamanism, spirit animals are known as power animals, meant to help, protect, educate, heal and inspire you on your life's journey. Each animal (guide) comes into your life for a purpose... which is why your spirit animal can change over time. There are also 4 types of spirit animals: messenger, journey, life and shadow spirit. Messengers show up to guide or warn you through a particular situation, and they will leave once that situation is over/solved. Journey spirit guides appear when you have a major decision to make in your life. Life spirit guides stay with your throughout your life (I believe the wolf is one of these for me). And the shadow spirit guide is the one to test you, specifically in areas that need changing.

I believe that one of my husband's animal spirit guides is the hummingbird. The hummingbird generally symbolizes joy, playfulness and adaptability. And every time we have moved into a new place, a hummingbird has shown up to greet him. Not only would it appear every morning for the first 3 days after we moved in, but it would hover right in front of my husband's face for a few moments, as if waiting to be acknowledged, then it would fly away… never to return again.

My son still believes that our cat was one of his personal spirit animals. They often seemed to commune in silence together. And though our cat was nice enough to all of us, even if he was in one of his cranky moods, my son could pick him up or pet him without getting growled at or scratched. He – the cat – even seemed to have an uncanny ability to be inside the house and suddenly outside of it without any of us opening the door for him.

Sometimes when I have a question that I've been asking God (aka the Universe), and I am open to receiving an answer, I get a message from an animal spirit. That is why I believe that the owl showed up in my life when it did. During the time that I was living in that home in Florida, I was continuously reading and studying all things having to do with spirituality. To me, that meant that I was on the right path and that I should continue doing what I was doing.

When we moved again a few years later, I had begun to doubt myself again. Then suddenly, once a night for 3 nights in a row, a skunk would spray right under my bedroom window! And when I finally looked up the symbolism of the skunk, I learned that it symbolized independence and self-respect. The little guy was telling me to have more faith in myself. And as soon as I received that message, the skunk never sprayed under my window again.

Another example: One day, while I was working at my office desk, which was temporarily in the living room, I heard a knocking sound. So I went to the front door and looked out – nothing. Then I heard it again – louder this time. Since I was busy, I chose to ignore it. But soon it got even louder. This time I looked out the window next to my desk… and lo and behold, there was a woodpecker hovering next to the porch railing! Once he noticed that I finally saw him, he looked right at me, hovering in front of the window for a few seconds, then flew away. I still swear to this day that he winked at me, though I know that is impossible.

When I looked up the symbolism for the woodpecker, I noticed that it often shows up in your life to let you know to use your intellect and discernment to follow through on your ideas… but also to seize the moment. And that was when I was considering expanding my business again! I never saw that woodpecker again after he gave me that message.

The same type of thing has happened to many people that I know. My son's high school teacher, for instance, told us that his father had always loved owls. And after he passed away, whenever he (the principal) would be going through a rough time, a huge owl would drop down onto his front lawn or right in front of his car, as if his father was sending him a message that he was watching over him and everything would be alright. How cool is that?

Most recently, was I was in the midst of writing this section, I was visited 3 times by a raven. Now, we have many different types of birds around our house: cardinals, crows, woodpeckers, bluebirds, blackbirds, turkeys, turkey vultures, even a few hawks and the occasional eagle… but I noticed the shadow of this bird a few days ago that seemed much bigger than the standard crow. When I saw him perch in a tree in the backyard, I said to him, "What type of bird are you?" He made some sort of noise, as if he was annoyed that I didn't know, then he flew further back onto one of our electrical wires closer to the street.

The next day, there he was again, while I sat on the back porch reading. He flew down onto the ground and appeared to look at me. The day after that, I was enjoying watching the sun go down in the back yard when he flew over my head in a circle at least 3 times, all the while making that same noise, as if he was actually trying to communicate with me. That's when I decided to go look up the meaning of the raven. And the 3 main aspects I was given were "synchronicity" (one of my favorite words), MAGIC, and healing. I had been feeling down about what my future might hold, but this was definitely an awesome message! Now I'm certain that I need to finish this book and get it out there for the right person/people to read. And I am looking forward to the future once again.

I never did see that raven again, by the way.

In general, over these past few years, I have also began to notice that if I respected the animals and insects around me – and wasn't afraid of them – they wouldn't bother me half as much as they used to. I realize that some of that was probably as simple as "what you resist persists," meaning you can choose to let something bother you or not, and this can apply to more than just annoying insects – but regardless, it does seem as if not worrying about bugs or flying insects reduces the instances where they bother me, while they harass everyone else around me. I've even tested it a few times by telling the occasional fly or other flying insect, "If you don't come near me, you get to live, but if you get in my face, I will have to kill you," and they always seem to disappear. Could it be that animals and insects are a lot like dogs, who can sense when you are afraid of them? Or maybe it has to do with the energy you admit when you are not afraid or angry. All I do know is that I can't remember the last time I got stung by a bee or had a mosquito bite. And that's fine by me.

My husband's diabetes gave him neuropathy in his legs. That made it difficult for him to notice if he got stung by a bee or bitten by a spider. The last time he got bitten by a brown recluse (a very poisonous spider), the wound on his inner thigh was bigger than a quarter by the time he noticed it. When we took him to the ER for them to treat him, the doctor said he would have to clean out the wound. But when he was going to numb the area, my husband told him not to bother; that he didn't feel it anyway. So the doctor started to clean it...only he couldn't seem to handle the fact that my husband didn't have any pain killers... he promptly turned green and left the room. He never came back. One of the nurses had to finish the job.

My husband is highly allergic to bees. One day, 3 bees of a particularly rare type stung him near his right eye! He was in a lot of pain, and could barely see for nearly a month. But once he had recovered, he no longer needed to wear his bifocals; his eyesight had actually <u>improved</u>!

4
HAVE NO FEAR

*"Worrying won't stop the bad stuff from happening,
it just stops you from enjoying the good."*
CHARLIE BROWN

For the last few years, I have noticed that in general, fear has become less and less a part of my life. Once I realized that God wasn't watching my every move to see if I was "sinning"… that I wasn't going to end up in Hell, since there isn't one… and that the Universe in general wasn't against me, so many of my fears seemed kind of fruitless. I didn't realize how many things I was afraid of until those fears started to dissipate. Now I can distinguish the difference between being concerned about something, and feeling fear over it. And that has vastly reduced the stress in my life.

For instance, on the Nature Preserve we lived on, our house was only a few yards away from a pretty big pond. And this pond had *alligators* in it. So we would occasionally have 4 to 6-foot alligators swimming in or sunning themselves next to the pond on any given day.

Now, I was born in New England, where alligators were never an issue. And I've seen enough reality TV shows to know what type of damage those creatures can do to a human body. Plus, I had 2 children to consider… and yet I was not afraid of sharing space with these creatures. It didn't even bother me that we were not allowed to shoot them (since they were protected under the laws of the Preserve).

Of course, we took precautions. We kept the grass all around the house mowed down so as not to give the alligators any reason to nest (the only reason they would attack us would be to protect their eggs). And we didn't swim in the pond – or the lake – as that was their territory. But as long as they stayed on the opposite side of the pond, we were fine with that. And they never came close to the house. It was a case of mutual respect.

I also used to have a terrible fear of thunder storms. Most of my life, I would cower under the covers whenever a storm would hit. But now I *revel* in such storms. Whenever a storm passes through the area, I just say "Thank you, Mother Earth, for cleansing us... and for keeping us protected." And I swear, whenever I do that, no matter how vicious the storm is at the time, it seems to lesson in intensity, if not dissipate all together. And we have never had issues with flooding, leaking roofs or even losing power for more than a few minutes. Whether it's pure coincidence or not, I am one of the few people I know who can sleep like a baby during a thunderstorm (and I am a very light sleeper otherwise).

Speaking of sleep, how many nights have you wasted worrying about what was going to happen in the future… even if that future was just the next day? It took me a long time to realize that worrying over what may or may not happen was a complete waste of my time… and energy. So if there happens to be something that I am concerned about, I do what I can do about it when I can, and if there is nothing left I can do before I go to bed, I stop thinking about it and go to sleep. Sometimes I will send some healing energy out to a friend or family member who needs it first, or ask my guardian angel (or the angels in general) to help out in a particular situation, but that is as far as I will let it go. I prefer to let my subconscious work on any problems while I'm asleep… and tackle the problem when I wake up the next morning.

I have also stopped worrying so much over finances. I grew up thinking that "money was the root of all evil", but no more. Money is just one means to an end in most circumstances. It's what you choose to do with it that makes it appear to be good or evil.

Money had almost ruined my marriage on more than one occasion in the past. I have not yet died from lack of money, no matter how often I thought that I would, so if it hasn't happened yet, I don't believe that it ever will. And once I started to think of money in terms of exchanging *energy* (something they talk about in *The Law of Attraction*), it doesn't bother me as much to spend it. Of course, I am not rich by any standard, but I know deep down that I will always have exactly what I *need*… if not always what I *want* (or *think* that I need.) For instance, we got a flat tire unexpected one day and we didn't have the money for a new one. My first reaction wasn't to gripe or complain, or think "Why always me?" like I used to do. Instead, I actually smiled and thought to myself "I wonder what adventure we're going to have now." And low and behold, we just happened to be driving by this automotive store we had never gone to before, and they were selling used tires… and they were having a sale. Wow.

That is the difference between worrying or not worrying… suffering or not suffering. Worry is just another form of fear, after all.

My brother's house was part of a community, and it had a pool that we frequented often. One evening we managed to get the pool to ourselves. We weren't in there long when we heard this really loud noise that sounded kind of like someone had pulled a huge lever that activated electricity. My husband yelled, "Get out of the pool – now!" so we did. As we were driving down the road in the golf cart back toward the house, we saw a charcoaled squirrel next to the telephone pool at the entrance to the pool. Apparently, said squirrel had nibbled on the wrong wire... and he took out half the community's electricity to boot! Our electric company told us later that if we hadn't seen that squirrel there, they could've taken many hours to figure out what the problem was, and we wouldn't have had electricity until the next day. We were also lucky we didn't get electrocuted in the pool, as that wire was close enough to have fallen into it.

Our cat loved to catch birds, mice and other rodents and leave them as prizes on our back porch. One day he caught a baby mole. But this time when he brought it us, it was still alive. He decided to play with it a bit before killing it. Only when he let it go, instead of running away, it simply dug into the ground and disappeared. The look at the cat's face was priceless; he was dumbfounded.

5

BFFs (Best Friends Forever)…. NOT!

*"Listen, Linus, friendship isn't about who you've
known the longest. It's all about the friend who comes
by and stands by your side in bad times."*
CHARLIE BROWN

When you are in high school, you think that the friends you have then you will have forever. There is just no way that anything could tear you apart.. or so you believe. Then you graduate. And most of your friends go away to college. Or *you* go away and they don't. You get full-time jobs, fall in love, get married, have children… and when you get that invitation to your first high school reunion 10 years later, you suddenly realize that you hadn't even thought of most of those people for…well, the last ten years.

It was the same for me. Sure, my closest friends and I started out by calling or writing to each other occasionally for the first year or so, but soon life and all its craziness intervened, the years went by, and we lost touch.

That was to be expected. It's the rare friendship that lasts past high school.

College is a bit different. Many of the friendships that are formed in college can stand the test of time. You are older and you tend to form friendships based on mutual likes and similar career goals. And that seemed to be the case for me. I had transferred to the big city in my junior year after spending the first two years in a small private Christian school; the transfer was necessary for me to fulfill the requirements for my major (which was Radio, TV & Film). It was quite a shock for me to live in a big city, as I had lived in small towns since I was 10 years old and my family had moved to the country. (I am definitely a country girl at heart.)

I met my best friend when she was a junior and I was a senior. She had requested to be my roommate the previous

135

semester when she had come to the city to visit the city campus. We hit it off right away. She was very different from me, which I liked: petite, with gorgeous long brown hair (she said she had been a model when she was younger), very independent, and quite boy crazy. But she also had a big heart and a great sense of humor. She was a Communications major, so we had that in common as well.

It was she who convinced me to try out my very first frat party – which wasn't such a hard sell, considering our dorm room was surrounded by fraternities. We would spend many weekends at this one frat around the corner that was a bit tamer than the rest. While she spent most of her time on the dance floor, I would be drinking the guys under the table in the corner (as beer didn't really seem to have much of an effect on me).

Eventually, I visited her home to meet her mother and brother (her father had passed before we met); we even spent a weekend in Atlantic City visiting her grandmother… where I got my first and only experience riding a 2-person bicycle.

She was my maid-of-honor when I got my married, and I was her maid-of-honor a few years later. We became godparents to each other's first-born children. Even though we never lived in the same state after I graduated, every time we spoke, no matter how long it had been since we had seen each other, it was like no time at all had passed.

It was a friendship that would last a lifetime.

Or so I thought.

Naturally, every relationship has its bumps in the road, and this one was no exception. But as the years went by, I started to feel a bit neglected. Even ignored. Part of it was that she had so many other friends, while I spent a lot of time home alone with my kids. But it was more than that. It wasn't so much that she would only call me whenever her husband was out of town (or at least when he was out of the house); or that when we'd visit each other, we always had to do what *she* had planned instead of what I wanted to do… as I truly was just happy just to spend time with her, however short that time was. But as cell phones, the internet and FaceBook became more and more the norm in our lives, for some reason neither of us could seem to write more than one email to the other every few months… if that. When staying in touch should have been as easy as sending a text message, that didn't seem to work for us… in her defense, it didn't help that I still do not own a cell phone.

But as my spiritual journey became more and more important in my life, it meant a lot to me to share it with someone… and I had thought that someone would be my best friend. Unfortunately, by the time we finally managed to get together again after my husband's accident, it may have been too late to fix a friendship that had been deteriorating (at least in my eyes) for quite some time.

I was so excited that my best friend was back in the country that when I got tickets to a concert for a band we had gone to together 20 years before, I thought she would jump at the chance to go with me. But she didn't. She was intent on coming down to Florida a few weeks earlier than that, in order to get out of the snow and get herself some sun. Though I was disappointed, I could understand her point; I had grown up in New England… I knew how stressful it was not to see the sun for weeks at a time.

Even so, the fact that she was coming raised my spirits. It had been at least 6 years since we had seen each other, so we had a lot of catching up to do. I even told her that she was welcome to brings her girls, as it would've been cool to have them and my boys get to know each other (the last time they had seen each other, they were very young children). But she opted to come on her own… and she brought her own agenda with her.

We only had 3 days and 2 nights together, but it seems from the start that she had every minute of those days planned out. Never mind that I had told her over the phone before she got here that I had no interest in going to the beach, or to any clubs (where the music would be too loud to talk), or to visit any of her relatives. Never mind that one of those days was actually my birthday and I intended to spend it with my family, not staying overnight at a hotel somewhere without them. Never mind that it felt as if we had lost touch, and I desperately wanted to rekindle that connection… and she didn't seem very interested in doing that.

So most of the time we were together, we spent it bickering over what we wanted to do. As usual, I ended up compromising more than I wanted to, but I was adamant about not going out partying (which meant drinking). That may have been something I was interested in doing with her 20-plus years ago, but not anymore. It didn't even seem to matter to her that I was allergic to cigarette smoke, and there would inevitably be people smoking at a night club. (The last time I had visited her home, we had gone to a club, and within minutes, I had become extremely ill due to the cigarette smoke that hovered over the dance floor.)

She didn't give up on trying to convince me to do things her way, though. Even as late as 10 o'clock at night – after my birthday cake had been eaten and everyone was settling in for the night – she still thought I would give in and take her out somewhere. When I refused, she got a bit ticked off… and spent the rest of the night telling my husband how much he had changed me. (Sorry to say, but my husband still hasn't forgiven her for that.)

I spent a lot of the time she was there hiding in the bathroom, trying not to let her see me cry. I was crying because I could feel the distance between us widening as the minutes ticked by. It seemed as if she didn't want to listen to me; as if sitting on the pier (since she insisted on getting a tan) and talking for more than an hour was more than she could bare. It was so obvious that she had other, more important things to do besides spend any quality time alone with me.

But the worst part for me was when I tried to explain to her about my spiritual journey. I was so excited to share that part of myself and all that I had learned since my husband's accident. But all she seemed to hear was that I no longer considered myself a Christian. Her first thought was "So you don't believe in God?"

"I never said that," I answered, disappointed. Why do so many people automatically think I'm an atheist because I don't follow a specific religion?

I was so shocked that I know I didn't explain myself very well.

After that conversation, things were even more awkward between us. She did try her best to help salvage things as well, but it was just too late.

It's not that we are no longer friends exactly… but we lost that easy connection we had always had.

Over the next few years, I've tried a few times to get it back… and I know that she has tried as well… but it was just gone. I still hear from her now and then, via email or FaceBook, but the communication is always brief. I wonder if I will ever stop missing my best friend.

I wish I could say that she was the only person I have lost since I left the religious fold. Even *before* my epiphany, I had a conversation with my son's therapist. This gentleman was a very enthusiastic man, who loved children and God… and not in that order. He actually carried his Bible with him everywhere he went, and nearly every other word out of his mouth was "praise God", "amen" or something of the sort. I had no problem with that at all. His care of my son was what mattered, and those two really did seem to have a connection.

Eventually, once he had come to our home a number of times, when his sessions with my son were done, he and I began to talk about things pertaining to God.. his favorite subject. I always loved a good spiritual conversation, and we had many good talks… until one day I said to him, "Have you ever considered that the Bible is just a book of myths, much like those in Native American culture, with stories meant to teach, instruct and inspire, and they aren't necessarily true?"

As he stood there, his mouth fell open… and it stayed that way for quite some time. I could tell he was completely dumbfounded; it was as if he had never for a second considered that that could be true.

I don't believe he ever answered my question. And from that day forward, he seemed to avoid me.

I'm sure my mother understood well before I did that I was not cut out to be the "good little Christian" she had brought me up to be. I guess the whole running-away-with-a-man-who-wasn't-my-husband thing kind of gave that away. I'm also sure that is why, when she was dying of cancer, she put her trust in my *sister* to be the Executor of her Will, even though I was her oldest child. (That hurt for a long time, to be honest.)

Just a few years ago, I also lost my biological sister... at least we no longer really speak to each other. That happened very unexpectedly, as I had no idea she had been holding back so many negative feelings toward me over the years. And one day she just decided to lay them all out at once. My first reaction was defensive, of course, as we both believed we were completely in the right about our perspective on things. But after a few days of going back and forth, with me trying to explain myself to her, watching her getting more upset with me instead of less, it suddenly hit me... in all the years we've known each other as adults, she has never actually supported me. Sure, she was a sounding board for me when I went through rough times, and we had plenty of conversations where we could agree on things – especially things having to do with other members of our family – but beyond that, she has never truly been there for me as a source of comfort. Nor has she ever visited my home, even when we lived less than 2 miles from each other (when our children were young). And I won't even go into the fact that her husband seems to hate me; I still have no idea why, other than the fact that he is a very hard person to like in general.

So why was I trying so hard to hold on to a relationship that wasn't edifying me? There was no give and take. And heaven forbid if I disagreed on a topic that she felt strongly about. There were quite a few subjects that I couldn't discuss with her at all, including politics and the state of the world... never mind religion. Though I can't help but think that the few things I did mention to her regarding how I felt in that area were what gave her the justification she needed to break things off with me.

Even so, after we hadn't spoken for a few months, I found out that one of our cousins was in the hospital again, and that the family didn't expect him to make it. The cancer had come back. It was then that I realized I had to tell my sister; since a lot of the people in my family don't speak to one another, I figured there was a good chance she hadn't heard, even though she lived only a few miles away from that side of the family. It was then I realized, to my surprise, that I actually wasn't holding a grudge against her. I knew we would never be close again, but she was still my sister and I still loved her… and she had a right to know. So I emailed her. She called me right back. The conversation was about my cousin – we didn't stray from that – but it was civil and grown up, and I could live with that.

Today we will speak to each other when the occasion warrants it – usually it's about family business – but the conversations are brief… and we don't get any more personal than we need to. I am sad about the loss of that relationship with my sister, but at the same time, I'm getting to the age where time is too short to spend it worrying about what others think… and I don't want to spend time with those who aren't on my side, family or not.

Ironically, this last move was to the South (I don't consider Florida the "real" South… more like it's the South for tourists), we moved to an area that is predominantly Christian (straight in the heart of the Bible Belt, as it were). Though it does seem as if most of the country is Christian of one denomination or another, this area is different. These people actually talk about God on a daily basis…out loud… with other people. Even people they don't know. I will hear "Have a blessed day," or "Praise God" or "I'll pray for you" quite often when I am out and about. This still amazes me, as growing up in New England, religion was treated as a very private thing… something to be kept to oneself, even within the family unit… with the exception of Christmas, weddings and funerals, when the God card could be taken out of hiding relatively safely. (In

New England, religion was up there with politics; it was something you discussed with those you did not know… or with family… at your own risk.)

These past few years, I have managed to find a few friends that I've been able to share my views on spirituality and religion with – though I do believe you can be religious as well as spiritual, most people tend to be one or the other. And though I have yet to find more than one person who agrees with me on any of my views, most of them are open enough to allow me to believe as I do without making it a major issue. Though I have found that many invitations to one-on-one get-togethers seem to get lost in the mail (so to speak) once most of them realize that I do not intend to go to church and that I am willing to consider alternative (meaning ways not written about in the Bible) ways of looking at the world.

I'm lucky that I have my oldest son to talk about spirituality with, though we often have differing opinions… and that's okay. I do still long for a female friend who I can discuss all of this with in person. I haven't given up hoping of finding that. Perhaps I will during my next 50 years.

Before my husband got out of rehab after his accident, we were pretty bad off financially. I had not attended a church for years, but I decided to go to the closest church to us, a block away. After the service, I approached the minister to ask him if the church could help us in any way. It turns out, the minister was also a registered nurse! And though he couldn't help us himself, he knew a woman in his congregation who had her own home health agency, and she agreed to help us. The church also gave a month's worth of food, and a few weeks later, the minister came over and built a ramp for our house so my husband could get in with his wheelchair. That woman is now one of our closest friends.

About a month after my husband got out of the hospital, we went to court for his Disability hearing. When we got to court, my husband saw the judge (while me and the boys stayed in the waiting room). The judge asked him to stand up and show him the extent of his injuries. The bailiff and the lawyer helped my husband out of his wheelchair and they dropped his pants. My husband told me that the judge took one look at his wounds and granted his disability, no more questions asked. The judge told him to expect a check in 60 days. We received it 3 days later... just in time to keep them from shutting off our electricity. I told my husband, "It's about time a man dropped his drawers for money."

6
THE INTERNET

As you have probably figured out by now, I grew up in a time before the Internet. I don't even believe I heard that word until I was in college. In the tenth grade, we had to take a mandatory computer programming class; I remember wondering why the hec it was a requirement.

Even in college, I typed up all of my essays on an electronic typewriter. (One of my side jobs was to type other students' essays at the end of year.)

Once I graduated from college and went into the work force, computers became more of a standard medium for typing letters and doing reports. It wasn't until a few years after that that email came into play. My oldest son was 2 years old when I got my very first AOL account, which was the hottest thing back then. I got this CD for AOL 1.0 in the mail and figured I'd give it a try. Before that, I had owned a computer, but I only used it to play games and do some writing.

I quickly became attached to this new mode of communication, spending hours after my kids were in bed visiting chat rooms and meeting people online from all over the world.

Eventually, chat rooms and the occasional Pogo game wasn't enough for me, so I began to branch out. I found a cool site on AOL for writers… teenagers specifically. I was actually "hired" by AOL as a NOVL Writer to provide editing services for those who wanted to learn how to write. It wasn't a paying position, but it was very rewarding.

Soon I graduated to Rainman Coder; I had to take classes to learn how to update and create the various screens on the AOL writing site. It was my very first experience with HTML coding. I started helping edit work written by adults as well.

Eventually, a gentleman whose book I had just finished editing mentioned that he had this cool idea for a business – to sell digital books. I had never heard of downloadable books, but I was intrigued. So I created a basic website using Dreamweaver, then I collected a few writers whose books I had edited and convinced them to let me publish their work as digital books… and we were off!

After a few months, I started to realize that this gentleman was very good at giving me ideas, but not so good at doing any of the actual work… nor had he volunteered to put up any money for this venture. So I dropped him and went off on my own. My company was one of the first digital publishing companies out there. Even before Amazon or Barnes & Noble sold eBooks, I was lucky not to have a lot of money for start-up costs, because so many other digital publishers put too much into marketing, merchant accounts and other start-up ventures, and with so little initial profit those first few years, they went belly-up pretty quickly. So I bought out one company… then another… and yet a third, taking the authors from each company with me, which allowed me to grow my business without much initial capital.

For the first 7 years, my company didn't make enough for the IRS to consider it more than a hobby, but that was okay with me, as I wanted to concentrate on taking care of my boys. Now and then I'd take on a part-time job as well, but this was my passion. And I seemed to be pretty good at it. I had to do everything, from the web design, to the accounting, to reading all the submissions, editing, marketing, as well as converting and formatting each digital book myself. I still do that to this day, both to save money and for the variety it gives me. Today my company has a backlist of over 250 titles, and with more than 350 eBooks for sale at any given time, nearly half of those also available in print. I have to say, I am quite proud of what I've managed to accomplish.

But I didn't just use the Internet for my business. Like so many others, I got hooked on the social aspects as well. First it was via MySpace, the hippest place in the virtual world… until that was replaced by FaceBook. What started out – for me – as a way to make as many "Friends" as possible eventually became way for me to feel as if I was part of the rest of the world while I took care of my children as a stay-at-home mom.

I will be forever grateful for this thing called the Internet, as it has given me a way to learn so much about the world... and most importantly, it's allowed me to meet many fascinating people, many of whom I now consider good friends, even if I have never met most of them in person. For quite a few years, while my husband was driving long-haul, coming home for a few days every few days, weeks, or months, it was the only way I could feel any connection to other adults, beyond the brief visits I would make to my mother's house – a house that was always filled with foster children.

The World Wide Web has been especially useful for me in my spiritual search, as the local libraries that I tend to live close to have a severely limited selection of books in that genre, and I just don't have the money to purchase all of the ones I'm interested in. So I visit YouTube often, and read blogs and articles on numerous topics, such as Reiki, meditation, Qigong, Tai Chi, the Law of Attraction, auras, chakras, tarot cards, spirit guides, soul mates, crystals, angels, psychics, empaths, Indigo children, quantum physics, spirit animals and so much more. The world really is an amazing place, and I love learning new things. I hope to never stop doing just that!

The Internet has taught me how important connection with others really is.

When our youngest son started to complain about his ears hurting one night, with his high pain tolerance, I knew it was already bad enough to take him to the ER, which I did. Only the ER was so packed that the triage nurse said it would be 6-8 hours before he could be seen. So I took him home and tucked him into bed; we would go back in the morning.

At 3am his brother woke me up and said that his little brother couldn't breathe. So I woke up my husband and this time we stormed the ER, demanding to be seen! They took us in, brought us to a bed in the back... and diagnosed my son with a respiratory infection and sent him home with antibiotics.

The next morning, while he was lying on the couch, I could SEE his heart pounding in his chest; it was going a mile a minute! This time, since it was a weekday, I took him straight to his pediatrician. The moment she put that little thing on his finger, she said, "His oxygen is at 20% - why didn't you take him to the ER?" I said, "They wouldn't SEE him!" I began to cry. The pediatrician called the ER. The hospital said he would have to come in by ambulance to be seen. The doctor's office was less than a mile from the ER. But we had to wait for an ambulance to come out and take our son back to the ER... where he waited in the hallway on a gurney for at least an hour.

A few hours later, the doctor told us he would have to be transferred to a hospital in Orlando. Thank God he was transferred, since they STILL didn't diagnose him correctly. He not only had pneumonia; he had a collapsed lung. He was there for 3 months.

7

I HAD A DREAM…

Growing up, I was never one to have bad dreams – or if I did, I don't remember them. With the exception of the talking heads that would visit me whenever my grandmother stayed overnight (or whenever I was very sick), my dreams were usually the stuff of fantasy, full of random people and places, with the occasionally celebrity thrown into the mix. The coolest ones to me were those in which I could fly. Though to this day I still wonder why I had to actually flap my arms to get airborne instead of flying the same way Superman did.

After I graduated from college, my dreams began to take on a theme similar to that in my waking state… namely, I'd be searching for something. The dreams started off innocently enough. For instance, I'd dream of being in my old elementary school… only it would be much bigger than I remembered… and I'd be wandering the halls, which were always full of people, some of whom I knew, but most of whom were strangers to me. I would rarely speak with any of them as I went on my way from hallway to hallway, upstairs and down, peeking into rooms, sometimes entering one, where various conversations or incidents were taking place. It was as if I was a bystander in my own dreams. I would dream of visiting my high school, and the same thing would happen. Or I might be in a mall, or a warehouse, an indoor/outdoor amusement park, a flea market…pretty much any place that could have connecting rooms.

As the years went by, my dreams seemed to incorporate more people I knew, some of whom I would actually speak to briefly, but for the most part it was as if I was an observer.

The strangest thing to me – and the coolest – was that I never visited the same type of building twice. Once I visited a haunted house, complete with scary lighting, red velour-covered furniture and the occasional skeleton or bat hanging on the walls, but for some reason I only wanted to see the attic. As

149

usual, there were people throughout the attic, all dressed appropriately in various "scary" costumes, as well as many interesting things to see, such as a huge piano with those pipes that go up to the ceiling, a bucket of apples, various antiques and tons of furniture covered in cloth. But I still wouldn't speak to anyone – though I don't recall being afraid to do so. Come to think of it, I wasn't afraid of being in the haunted house in the first place.

Another time I dreamed I was in a huge farmhouse. One room was completely filled with water, from the floor to the very high ceiling… and a kitten was in the room, floating inside for all the world as if it could swim. So I floated there with her as well, without having to take a breath of air. That was a very cool dream.

After I left my first husband, he would occasionally appear in my dreams. He would never speak to me; he'd just show up behind a tree or around the column of a building (in these dreams I was always outside), as if he was following me. But he never approached me. I interpreted this as a way of dealing with my guilt over how I left him; I knew I would one day have to have closure on that issue.

After my mother passed, I don't remember a lot of what happened that year, but I do know that I missed her terribly. I went through the various stages of grief during this time – denial, anger, bargaining, depression and acceptance. It was during the anger phase that I started to dream about her. I remember yelling at her in those dreams; I was so very angry at her for leaving us. (I still believe that if she had taken the time to take care of herself, instead of spending so much time caring for others, that she would still be alive today.)

My mother never replied to any of my fits of temper. She would just look at me, without expression, as if she knew I had to get it out of my system. Even then, a part of me believed that that was really my mother, visiting me in my dreams to let me know she was okay.

As the years went by, my mother would occasionally show up in one of my other theme-based dreams. She'd usually be standing with a few other women, all who would be talking with her, but they'd ignore me… acting as if I wasn't even there… though I could tell my mother knew that I was nearby. In these dreams she looked happier – at peace, even.

After my husband's accident, these theme-based dreams began to increase, and become much more interesting. In one dream, I walked inside a huge treehouse. As I climbed the stairs, there would be doors on each level/turn. All the doors would be open, and there would be people inside. Again, I would not speak to any of them – or if I did, I cannot remember. Some of the people would be friends or old classmates, but most of them were total strangers going about their business.

Another time I visited a fun house, only this one was both indoors and outdoors. And there was a small waterway that traveled between them, with buckets you could sit in to travel from place to place. As I floated through the park, I could see crowds of people, all going about their business. My mother was in that dream, and though she never looked at me, I could tell that she knew I was there.

I saw my father in a large concert hall… the building was round with hallways that could fit a truck, and many doors jutting out on one side. He was there with my step-mother, who I had yet to meet at that point. My mother was in the building as well, but try as I might, I could not get her to come with me to meet with my father.

Many people will say that dreams are windows to our subconscious. They are both a way for us to find answers to questions we are asking in our waking state, or ways to solve problems that are a bit too complicated for us to deal with in reality. But I tend to believe that they are way more than that… and that was confirmed by my life coach one day when I told her about one of my dreams. She explained that many of our dreams, especially those that are the most vivid, can be messages from the "other side", whether from Spirit (aka God/the Universe/Creator), or from loved ones who have passed. Once she said this, my theme-based dreams took on a whole new meaning for me. It was so cool to think that my mother was checking in on me now and then!

She also said that dreams that incorporate buildings tell us a lot about our spiritual journeys – and I have confirmed this information via numerous sources, both online and in books. Many religions also believe this. I was thrilled to think that while I was asleep, I was continuing my spiritual journey… especially when I learned that the level you are on in your dreams is significant. According to various sources, to see a building in your dream represents the body or self, and how high you are in the building represents your level of spiritual understanding or awareness. In most of my dreams, I was either in a one-floor structure or I was climbing to a higher level. To me, this could only be a good thing.

Have you ever had a dream that felt so real that you just knew it really happened? How is that possible, you may ask? Simple – there's a good chance that it did. One night I had this incredible dream; the kind where you wake up and immediately want to go right back. In this dream, I was standing at the top of a penthouse. The roof's floor was entirely covered in water, with these small, round areas to stand in between that were just big enough to hold a few chairs or a bed. The beds had sheer white curtains around them, much like mosquito netting, only sheer and flowing around them in the gentle breeze. And in between these areas flowed water, giving the impression of privacy for each area.

I was wearing a long white robe and I was barefoot. I walked slowly from section to section – no one was on any of these areas, strangely enough. I stepped over the water as if I had been doing it for years. And gliding through this tributary was a 30-foot snake! It was at least 3 feet in diameter. And the most amazing part about it… I was not at all frightened. I felt as if this snake was under my power, and I knew it would never hurt me.

When I woke, I was depressed; I wanted to go back and see what happened next.

My life coach had told me that there was a good chance that this dream was more than a dream… that it was me remembering who I had been in one of my past lives. It certainly *felt* real. And come to think of it, I believe I was a man in that dream as well. And I was very powerful. And boy, did I enjoy that feeling!

After she mentioned past lives, I recalled having a dream about my youngest son in which he was a warrior in Scotland some time many, many years ago. In that dream he had red hair, and he was very large – I believe he was a warrior sent to protect me. He couldn't speak in that dream either.

My life coach said that most likely I was recalling a past life in which my son had been my protector… and that he had been so in many of my past lives… and that in this lifetime I was mean to return the favor by being *his* protector. Who's to say if this is true or not, but I certainly like the idea.

I've always wondered which of my dreams were just my subconscious having fun with me and which of them were messages from the other side. And what if some of them are memories from my past lives? All I know is that there is a reason we have dreams… and those who rarely dream usually exhibit anti-social behaviors (scientific fact). So it cannot hurt to pay attention to our dreams – write them down whenever possible – as you never know what they can tell you.

One of the best examples of this I can give is the last one I had with my mother in it. In this dream, I was back in the house I had grown up in. It looked the same as it did when I was in high school. My father was in the kitchen with me – without his new wife. I didn't want to speak to him, as in real life we had not spoken to each other for years at this point. Suddenly, my mother popped into the room; one moment she wasn't there, and the next she was. She looked at me, then at my father. Again, she didn't speak, but I knew that she wanted me to talk to him. I shook my head. Then I turned and walked upstairs to my bedroom… where she promptly popped in to stand in front of me again. She turned her head, as if listening to my father as he was talking downstairs.

I sighed in resignation and said "Yes, mom, I'll talk to dad." She smiled and popped back out of the room.

When I woke up, the first thing I remembered was that mom had told me it was time to talk to my father. And when I searched inside of myself, all the hurt and anger I had toward him was gone… it had disappeared along with the dream. So I called him.

Today we are not exactly the best of friends, but we are on speaking terms. We can even occasionally have an interesting conversation. And there is no way you are going to tell me that my mother didn't visit me that night to give me the message to heal the rift between my father and I.

Once my husband had recovered enough that he could stand again, we knew it was time for us to move, though my brother was okay with us staying in his house as long as we needed to. I told my husband there was no way, with our credit, and the fact that he wasn't working, that we would find another place to live in this economy. Yet when we found the place we wanted, the landlords chose us over multiple applicants, for the simple fact that my husband was receiving Disability... because, they said, they knew that they wouldn't have to worry about him losing his job in this economy... that disability meant a steady income. That certainly was a pleasant surprise. We moved in 10 days later.

The day after my husband got his new glasses, he decided to go fishing on the pier in the lake nearby. That afternoon, he came back without his glasses. When I asked him what happened, he explained that he was walking back toward the golf cart with a fish on his pole... when our daddy owl suddenly came out of the woods and snatched the fish right off of it... and took his glasses along with it!

8

ALL THE WORLD'S A STAGE…
OR RATHER A MOVIE SET

When I was in high school, I decided that I wanted to be an actress. Some of my most enjoyable moments came from watching entire worlds unfold before me on the screen. And wouldn't it be so cool to know what it felt like to be someone else, if even for a little while? My own life wasn't half as interesting, in my opinion. So it should come as no surprise to those who know me that there were 3 movies that had a drastic effect on my life.

The first movie that set my life in a specific direction was STAR WARS: A NEW HOPE (1977). It was the 4th of July and it was raining so hard that fireworks were out of the question. So my parents took us to the movies. As I sat there, enveloped in a world of space ships, androids, Jedi knights and Wookies, I was entranced. *This* is what I wanted to do with my life; make movies that could transport you into an entirely different world. I vowed right then and there to become a cinematographer. I wanted to be the next George Lucas. That is why I chose the degree "Radio, TV & Film" when I went to college instead of going to an all-girls school to learn how to be a secretary like my father wanted me to.

Of course, as I look back on that movie, I realize that the message "May the Force be with you," had also began a spark inside of me… that even in a universe as vast as the Empire, someone as insignificant as a simple farm boy can make a difference.

I was living in Florida with my first husband when I saw this next movie. My life was stuck in a major rut when the movie POINT BREAK (1991) with Patrick Swayze was released. For some reason I had gone to see this movie by myself that day. Forget the fact that Swayze and Keanu Reeves were two of the hottest actors out at the time; it was the

157

movie's *message* that completely changed my life. Ironically, I had no desire to surf, nor to become an FBI agent. But here were two men living in completely different worlds, with vastly different world views, and they were learning from one another. As the FBI agent was getting to know the criminal for who he really was, he began to realize that there was much more to life than following all the rules that society created. It may not have been the best choice to rob banks, of course, but somehow the surfer's philosophy of life made much more sense. Because life was not worth living unless you lived it on the edge. "You want the ultimate, you've gotta be willing to pay the ultimate price," said Brodi (aka Swayze). He, too, could not stand the thought of being kept in a cage – whether that cage was actually a jail cell or the cubicle in some office building.

After I saw this movie, I knew that I had to get out of Florida; that I was not going to find what I wanted out of life living where I was. And within a few weeks, my first husband and I had packed our bags and we were on our way back East, with a plan for me to join the Army.

You can probably guess movie I will name last: CONVERSATIONS WITH GOD (2006). One man – ironically around the same age that I am now – was at his lowest point, searching for answers to life's biggest questions: "Who am I?" "Why am I here?" "What does God want from me?" It was then that my spiritual journey began in earnest.

One of my authors was an historical consultant. So I figured I would ask him if he could help me with some details about the time period I was writing my first book in. So I sent him an email. It turns out he was on the set of a movie that day, waiting for the rain to stop so filming could resume. Then he wrote "I'd love to help you with your book. I'm sitting here next to Brad Pitt and he's not very happy about all this rain." My eyes widened. I replied right back, asking him for more details. But instead of my author replying to me, Brad Pitt himself replied. He called me "Miss Debi" and asked if he could "read my pages." Hell, yeah! So I sent him the first 3 chapters of my book. My author said that he read them and he liked it. <puff up>

Our new home was on a Nature Preserve. We were not allowed to hunt or otherwise hurt any of the animals living there; with the exception of the wild hogs, since they were over-populating the area. My office window was only a few yards from the pond in our yard... where alligators took to sunbathing on the opposite end. I was never nervous about the alligators... we stayed out of each other's way... until the day my husband and I were roaming the area in our golf cart, and we saw the one gator that we had permission to kill. Well, I only saw his eye... it was slinking down into the water in our landlord's pond... and that eye was the size of a baseball! That gator was over 16 feet long... and it was not afraid of humans. That was when I knew it was time for us to move.

WORDS OF WISDOM
From Linus Van Pelt

"There's no heavier burden than a great potential."

When I was in grade school, I got a C in Algebra. My parents were quite upset. And yet when my younger sister got a C in math as well, they didn't seem especially concerned. When I asked my mother about it, she said "She did the best she could; we know you can do better." What's up with that?

"Never worry about tomorrow, Charlie Brown. Tomorrow will soon be today, and before you know it, today will be yesterday. I always worry about the day after tomorrow."

We spend so much time worrying about what might happen, don't we? It took me many years, but I have finally realized that worrying is a wasted emotion. That's not to say that you don't care what happens to you or the people you love. If there is something you can do to make sure someone does not get hurt or into trouble, by all means, do whatever it takes. But worrying is not going to solve any problems or stop something from happening. So instead of worrying, I say a prayer of protection over myself or those I care about, and then let it go, as best I can.

"I guess it's wrong always to be worrying about tomorrow. Maybe we should think only about today…"

This goes with my philosophy that there is only NOW.
'Nuff said.

IN SUMMARY…

"Sometimes I lie awake at night and I ask
'Is life a multiple choice test or it is a true or false test?'
Then a voice comes to me out of the dark, and says
'We hate to tell you this, but life is a thousand word essay.'"
CHARLIE BROWN

Our world is on the cusp of an evolutionary shift… Christianity's term for it would be "the end times." I no longer believe this means that the devil will rise and we will have 1000 years of doom and gloom as the Bible predicts. But I do believe that this is where we will either destroy ourselves as a species or move on to another plane of existence. We could very well create a "Heaven on Earth" if everyone would stop long enough to listen to that still, small voice – which many call God – inside of them.

Do you realize that religion is the only thing that hasn't evolved in the last millennium? There is something inherently wrong about that, don't you think? That is why human beings treat each other so horribly. Most people are desperately trying to fill a void inside of themselves by outside sources…. whether it be via the acquisition of money, power, drugs, alcohol, or material things. But the world cannot be saved by political, economic or religious means. It can only be saved if we all realize that everything we do effects everyone else… that we are all one… all connected. Even science is starting to realize what spirituality has known all along… that we are all energy, and made up of the same stuff. It is up to each of us to follow our own spiritual paths… and to help others find theirs as well. We – meaning all humans – need to realize that God is talking to us all the time, in millions of ways.

Even Charles Schultz realized this fact more than 60 years ago when he began his revolutionary cartoon called *Charlie Brown*. Rather than the typical cartoons of the day, that were filled with slapstick comedy or adventure, Mr. Schultz decided to create a cartoon that tells the truth about life. And he did this through the ordinary exchanges between a young boy named Charlie Brown and his friends… and of course, his dog. Though most of us tend to believe that those big events – graduations, weddings, the birth of our children, the purchase of our first homes – are what give our lives meaning, it's actually those little, every day, *ordinary* moments that tend to shape and mold us the most profoundly. And it's the people in our lives that create those ordinary moments with us.

Most of us live ordinary lives. We may even be amazed to hear that someone thinks of us as *more* than ordinary. I know that I have felt this way the few times someone has referred to me as special in one way or another. But ironically, living an ordinary life is really anything *but* ordinary. Because in our search for the biggest answers in life to questions such as "Is there life after death?" and "Is there a God?", "What is my purpose?" are usually found in the midst of those little *ordinary* moments.

I hope you've learned as much about yourself as you have about me… and that you will come back in another 50 years to read how it all turned out.

Debi Staples

\

"In the book of life's questions,
The answers are not in the back."
CHARLES SCHULTZ
Creator of *Charlie Brown*

CHARLIE BROWN
"Someday, we will all die, Snoopy."

SNOOPY
"True, but on all the other days, we will not."